# CROSS WORDS

## FOR

# BRIGHT SPARKS

Puzzles and solutions by

Dr Gareth Moore

B.Sc (Hons) M.Phil Ph.D

Illustrations by Jess Bradley

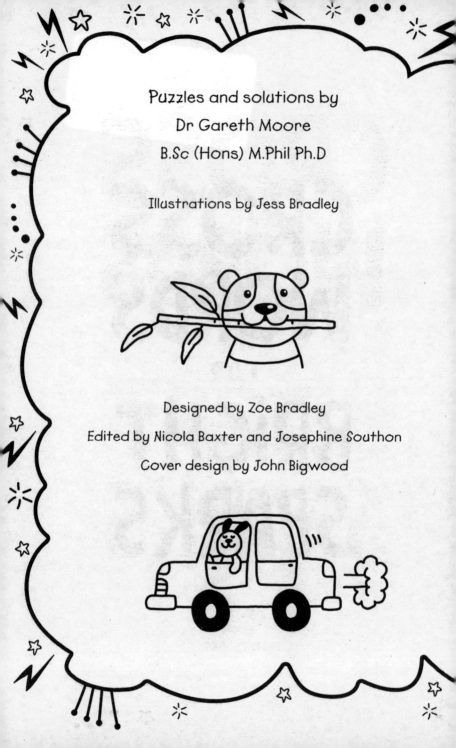

Designed by Zoe Bradley

Edited by Nicola Baxter and Josephine Southon

Cover design by John Bigwood

# CROSS WORDS

## FOR

# BRIGHT SPARKS

BUSTER BOOKS

First published in Great Britain in 2019 by Buster Books,
an imprint of Michael O'Mara Books Limited,
9 Lion Yard, Tremadoc Road, London SW4 7NQ

W www.mombooks.com/buster   f Buster Books   🐦 @BusterBooks   📷 @buster_books

Puzzles and solutions © Gareth Moore 2019

Illustrations and layouts © Buster Books 2019

A CIP catalogue record for this book is available from the British Library.

ISBN: 978-1-78055-629-1

7 9 10 8 6

This product is made of material from well-managed, FSC®-certified
forests and other controlled sources. The manufacturing processes
conform to the environmental regulations of the country of origin.

This book was printed in November 2023 by
CPI Group (UK) Ltd, Croydon, CR0 4YY.

MIX
Paper | Supporting
responsible forestry
FSC® C171272
FSC
www.fsc.org

# INTRODUCTION

Crosswords are the perfect puzzle challenge for bright sparks and this book is packed with over 100 of them. They are divided into four levels of difficulty, so you can start as a rising star and quickly gain scintillating supernova skills.

Your mission is to write a letter in each white square, so that you end up with a grid full of words. Some of the letters you enter will be part of only one word, while others will appear in two criss-crossing words – which is why the puzzles are called **cross**words!

The clues for each grid are divided into **across** clues, which read left to right, and **down** clues, which read top to bottom. Each clue has a number that tells you which square in the puzzle the answer should start in.

Each clue also has a bracketed number: (3).
It tells you how many letters are in the answer.

Once you have solved a clue, write the word in. If you think of more than one possible answer, try some of the words that cross over it to see which fits.

Sometimes a clue has two parts, divided by a semi-colon (;). Both parts give the same answer. You may also see underscores, like this: '_ _ _'. This means you need to find a word that will fit into the gap.

Use a pencil to fill in your answers, then you can change them if you need to.

If you get stuck on any clue, try asking a grown-up for help. If you're REALLY stuck, the answers are at the back of the book for you to take a sneak peek!

There's also a 'Time' box at the bottom of each puzzle page, so you can record how long each puzzle takes you to complete.

Happy puzzling!

## Introducing the Crosswords Master:
## Gareth Moore, B.Sc (Hons) M.Phil Ph.D

Dr Gareth Moore is an Ace Puzzler and author of many puzzle and brain-training books.

He created an online brain-training site called BrainedUp.com, and runs an online puzzle site called PuzzleMix.com. Gareth has a Ph.D from the University of Cambridge, where he taught machines to understand spoken English.

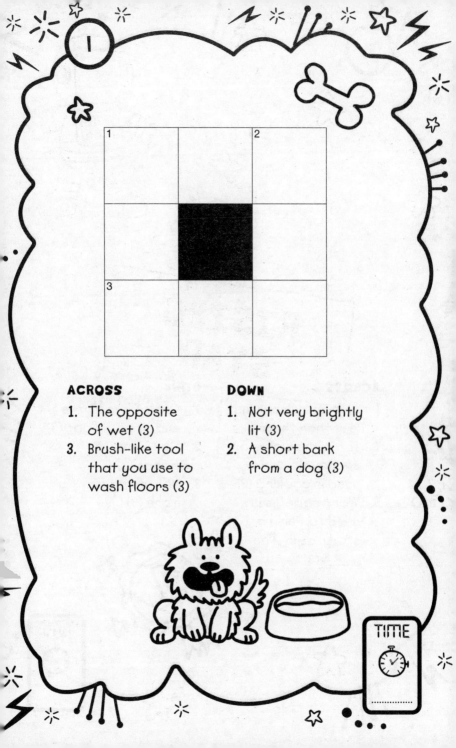

**1**

|   |   |   |
|---|---|---|
| 1 |   | 2 |
|   | ■ |   |
| 3 |   |   |

## ACROSS

1. The opposite of wet (3)
3. Brush-like tool that you use to wash floors (3)

## DOWN

1. Not very brightly lit (3)
2. A short bark from a dog (3)

TIME

**2**

|   |   |   |
|---|---|---|
| ¹ | ² | ³ |
| ⁴ |   |   |
| ⁵ |   |   |

## ACROSS

1. An even number just less than three (3)
4. It might be olive or sunflower, and is used in cooking (3)
5. Word sometimes used to finish a story, as in 'The ____' (3)

## DOWN

1. One of five at the end of your foot (3)
2. Come first in a race (3)
3. Not young any more (3)

TIME

.............

|   |   |   |
|---|---|---|
| 1 | 2 | 3 |
| 4 |   |   |
| 5 |   |   |

## ACROSS

1. Metal fastening you might use to attach paper to a board (3)
4. A value of playing card; also an expert (3)
5. Drops of water formed on cool surfaces during the night (3)

## DOWN

1. A pile of blank paper joined together at one edge (3)
2. Frozen water (3)
3. The opposite of old (3)

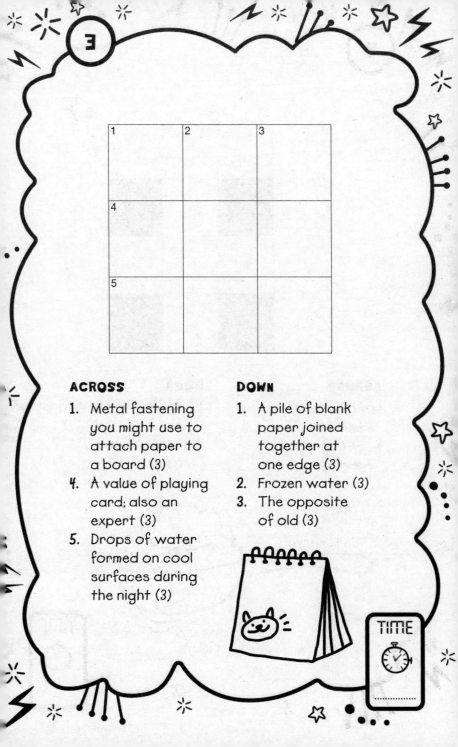

TIME

## ACROSS

1. Gentle; not hard (4)
3. On top of; above (4)

## DOWN

1. A place where things can be bought (4)
2. Give food to a person (4)

TIME

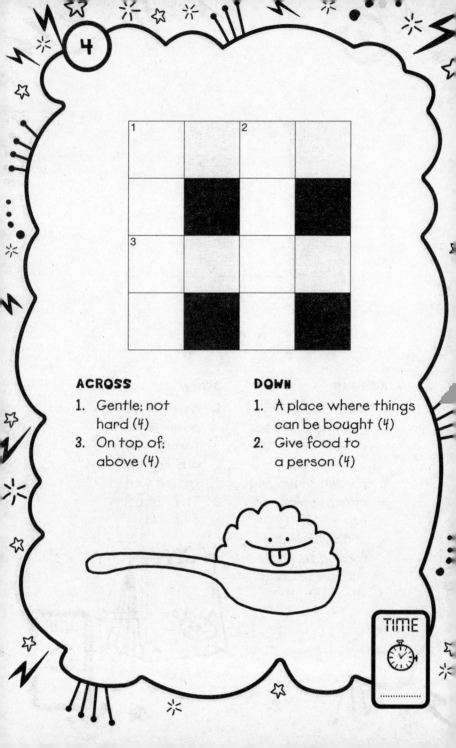

## ACROSS

3. Painful or aching, like your throat when you have a cold (4)
4. A single movement of one leg in front of the other while walking (4)

## DOWN

1. A floating vessel, such as a ship (4)
2. Hold on to, rather than give away (4)

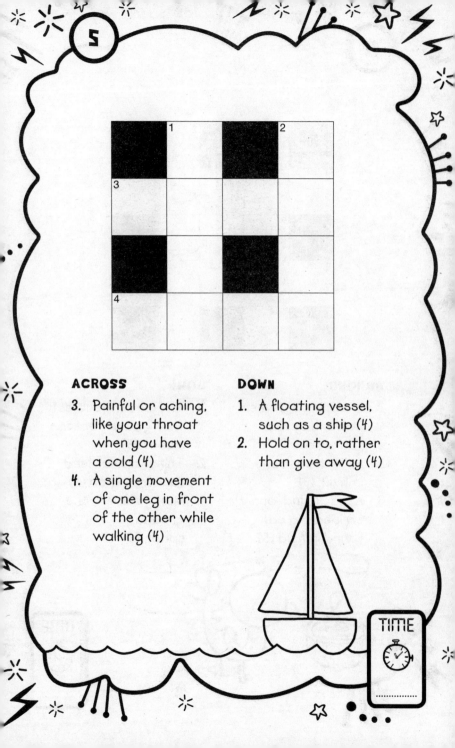

TIME

## ACROSS

3. It comes between yesterday and tomorrow (5)
5. Small seed found in fruit (3)
6. A black-and-orange striped big cat, found in Asia (5)

## DOWN

1. The current subject that you are talking about (5)
2. Thin material used for writing on (5)
4. Make a hole in the ground with a spade (3)

TIME

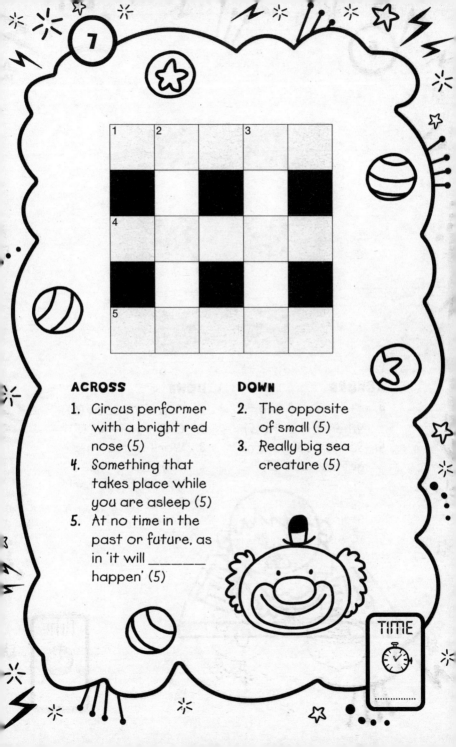

| 1 | 2 | | 3 | |
|---|---|---|---|---|
| | | | | |
| 4 | | | | |
| | | | | |
| 5 | | | | |

**ACROSS**

1. Circus performer with a bright red nose (5)
4. Something that takes place while you are asleep (5)
5. At no time in the past or future, as in 'it will _____ happen' (5)

**DOWN**

2. The opposite of small (5)
3. Really big sea creature (5)

TIME

## ACROSS

4. The time of day when it is dark (5)
5. Someone who is not yet an adult (5)

## DOWN

1. Tap on a door (5)
2. One more time (5)
3. Work at learning something, like you might do for a test (5)

TIME

...........

## ACROSS

1. Horse's foot (4)
4. Small stick struck to create a flame (5)
5. Just the one time (4)

## DOWN

1. Place where a person lives (4)
2. Many times; frequently (5)
3. Outer covering for your foot (4)

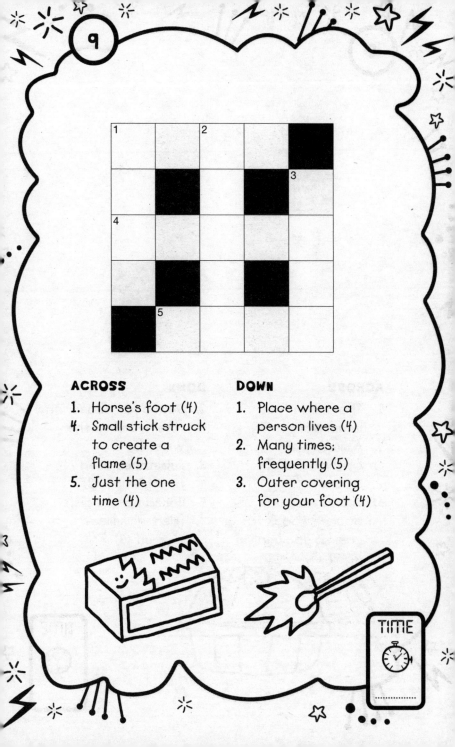

TIME

## ACROSS

1. Short, thin tree branch (4)
4. A single part of the head of a flower (5)
5. Sound that has bounced back to you, so you hear it again (4)

## DOWN

2. Device for measuring time, worn on the wrist (5)
3. Substance used to style hair (3)
4. Baked pastry dish filled with meat or fruit (3)

TIME

## ACROSS

1. Hurt or damage (4)
3. Rain falls from it (5)
4. Something you eat (4)

## DOWN

1. Something you say when you meet someone (5)
2. Shaped like a circle (5)

TIME

## ACROSS

4. Something attached to an item to say who owns it (5)
5. The number of dwarfs that Snow White met (5)

## DOWN

1. Group of children at school who are taught together (5)
2. Higher up than (5)
3. Tree, bush or flower, for example (5)

Mine!

TIME

**13**

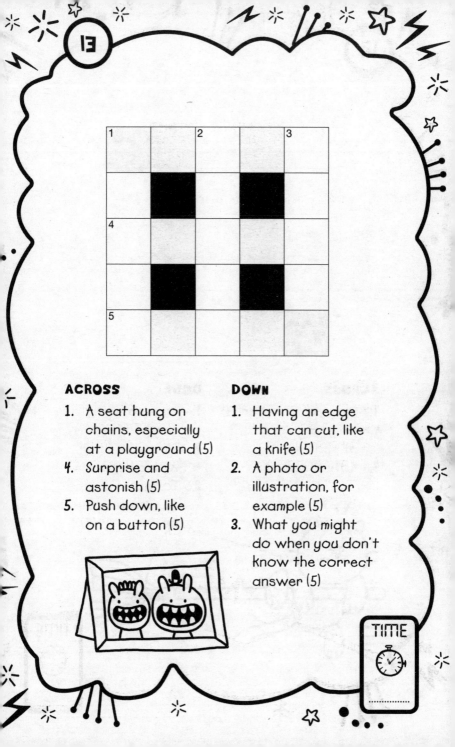

## ACROSS

1. A seat hung on chains, especially at a playground (5)
4. Surprise and astonish (5)
5. Push down, like on a button (5)

## DOWN

1. Having an edge that can cut, like a knife (5)
2. A photo or illustration, for example (5)
3. What you might do when you don't know the correct answer (5)

TIME

................

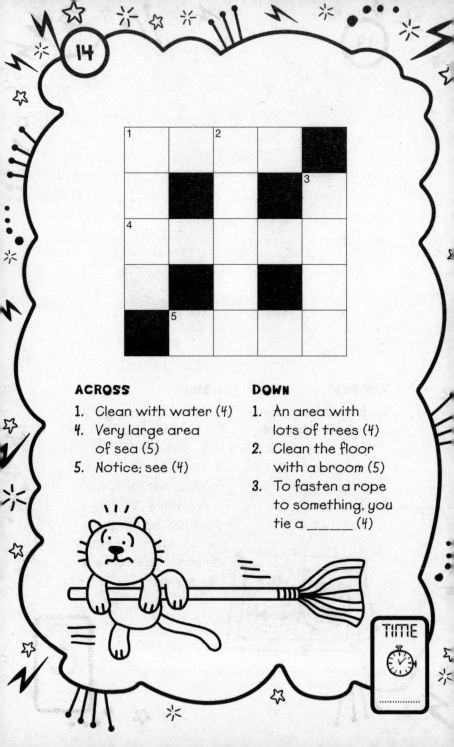

**ACROSS**

1. Clean with water (4)
4. Very large area of sea (5)
5. Notice; see (4)

**DOWN**

1. An area with lots of trees (4)
2. Clean the floor with a broom (5)
3. To fasten a rope to something, you tie a _____ (4)

TIME

...............

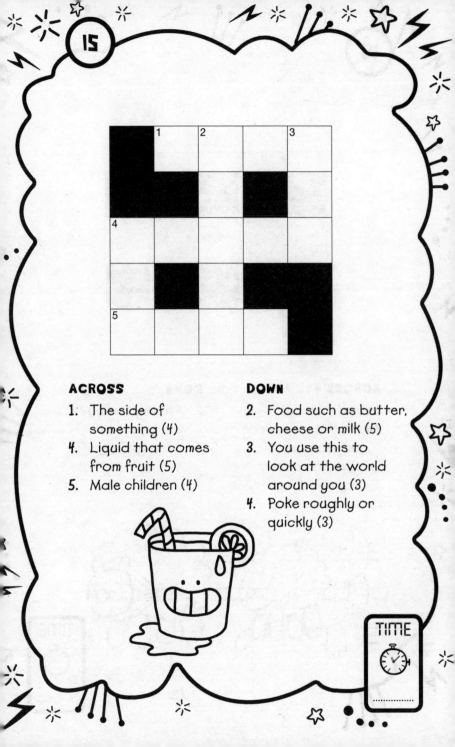

## ACROSS

1. The side of something (4)
4. Liquid that comes from fruit (5)
5. Male children (4)

## DOWN

2. Food such as butter, cheese or milk (5)
3. You use this to look at the world around you (3)
4. Poke roughly or quickly (3)

TIME

..................

## ACROSS

1. Not true (5)
4. Think the same as someone else (5)
5. Catches a foot on something and then falls over (5)

## DOWN

2. Strong feeling of annoyance (5)
3. They go 'baa' (5)

TIME

## ACROSS

1. What you might read in a daily paper (4)
4. Something added to drinks to make them sweeter (5)
5. Arriving after the planned time (4)

## DOWN

2. Of exactly the same value (5)
3. The beginning of a race (5)

TIME

...................

## ACROSS

1. Iron, silver or copper, for example (5)
4. It's between yellow and blue in a rainbow (5)
5. Grab hold of a ball in the air (5)

## DOWN

1. Conjuring tricks, such as making something vanish (5)
2. Special reward (5)
3. Midday meal (5)

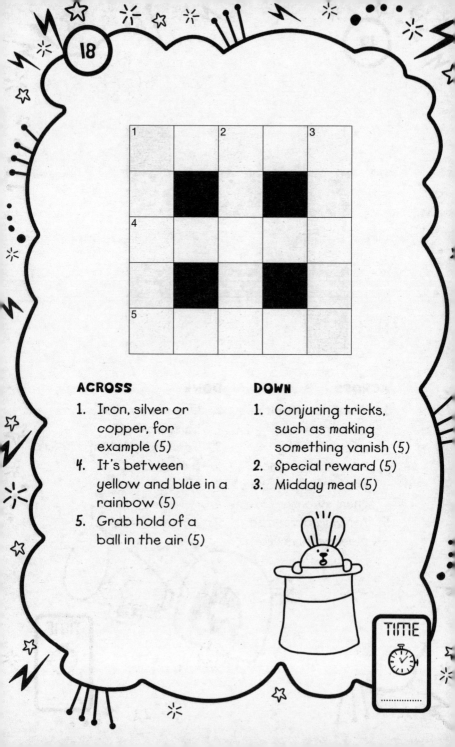

TIME

..............

## ACROSS

3. Precious stone, like you might find in a ring (5)
5. Briefly put something into liquid and then take it back out (3)
6. Very large bird of prey (5)

## DOWN

1. Prize given for bravery, or for winning (5)
2. Answer a question (5)
4. Hairpiece worn on your head (3)

TIME

## ACROSS

4. The opposite of over; beneath something (5)
5. Phones someone up (5)

## DOWN

1. Really fast (5)
2. A fully grown person (5)
3. Powdery ice on the ground (5)

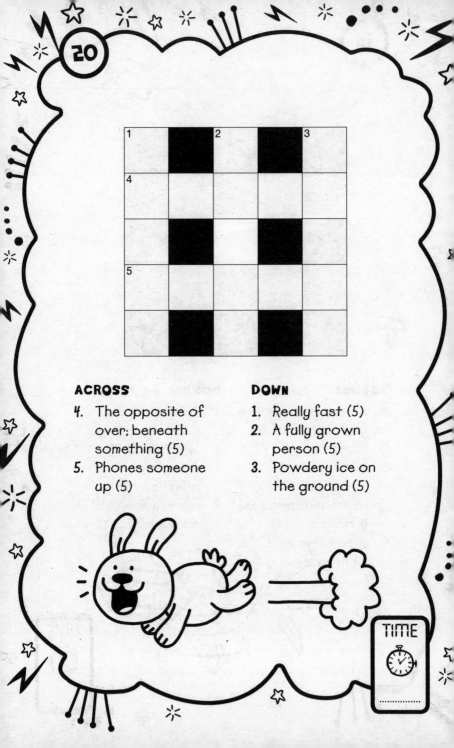

TIME

## ACROSS

1. Spare-time activity (5)
4. Bitter, yellow fruit, sometimes added to cola or other cold drinks (5)
5. Bamboo-eating animal (5)

## DOWN

2. A play set to music all the way through, such as Mozart's "The Magic Flute" (5)
3. Wide, like a river (5)

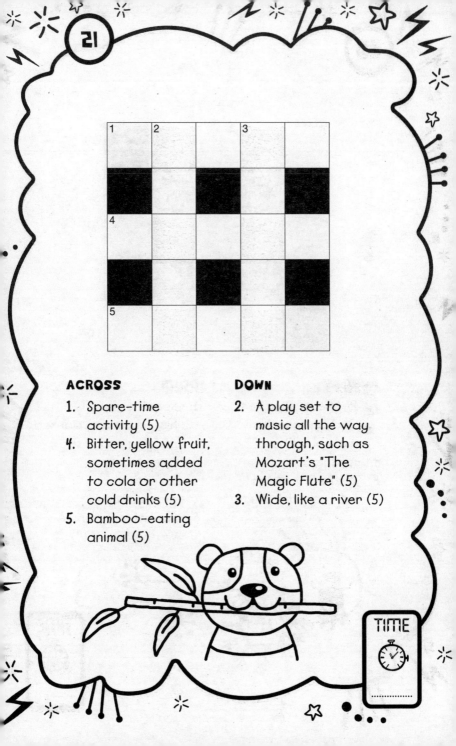

TIME

**22**

## ACROSS

1. Retrievers, collies and poodles, for example (4)
4. A fang (5)
5. White flakes that fall from the sky (4)

## DOWN

1. Specific day in history; a day marked on a calendar (4)
2. Deep moan to express annoyance (5)
3. Something you watch on TV (4)

TIME

....................

## ACROSS

1. A dull, continuous pain (4)
3. Hot; very spicy (5)
4. Plant with green, feathery leaves called fronds (4)

## DOWN

1. Not yet dead (5)
2. Wading bird with long, thin legs (5)

TIME

## ACROSS

1. A feeling that makes you want to scratch (4)
4. Not very happy (5)
5. You see the world using these (4)

## DOWN

2. One of the body's five main senses (5)
3. The opposite of cold (3)
4. Purpose, as in 'what do you ____ it for?' (3)

TIME

**ACROSS**

1. Flickering part of a fire (5)
4. You might use this for drawing straight lines (5)
5. Tall, narrow building (5)

**DOWN**

1. Position before second and third (5)
2. Give permission for (5)
3. Something wrong; a mistake (5)

TIME

## ACROSS

1. Thin fog, sometimes seen by water (4)
4. Something you might set to wake you up in the morning (5)
5. What a door is when you can walk through it (4)

## DOWN

2. A house built from blocks of snow (5)
3. The number of sides a triangle has (5)

TIME

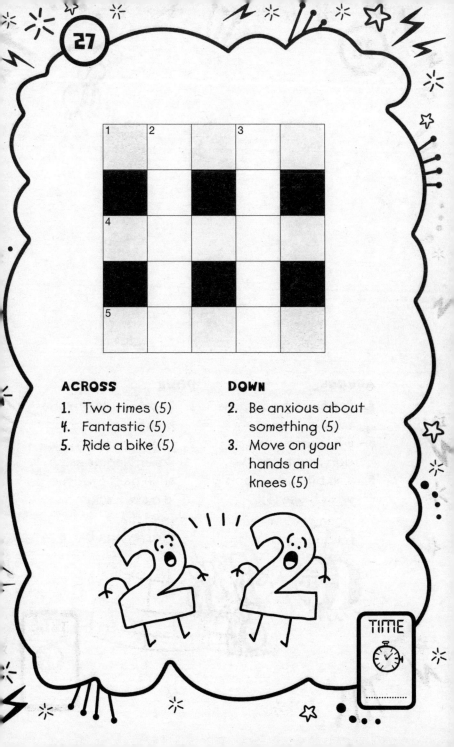

## ACROSS

1. Two times (5)
4. Fantastic (5)
5. Ride a bike (5)

## DOWN

2. Be anxious about something (5)
3. Move on your hands and knees (5)

TIME

## ACROSS

3. Someone who poses for photos (5)
5. Bite sharply, like a dog might do (3)
6. You bite your food with these (5)

## DOWN

1. Food product made by bees (5)
2. How far down something goes, such as the water in a swimming pool (5)
4. Stop living (3)

TIME

..............

## ACROSS

4. Picture taken with a camera (5)
5. More of something (5)

## DOWN

1. How fast something is moving (5)
2. Path to take to get somewhere (5)
3. Adult girl (5)

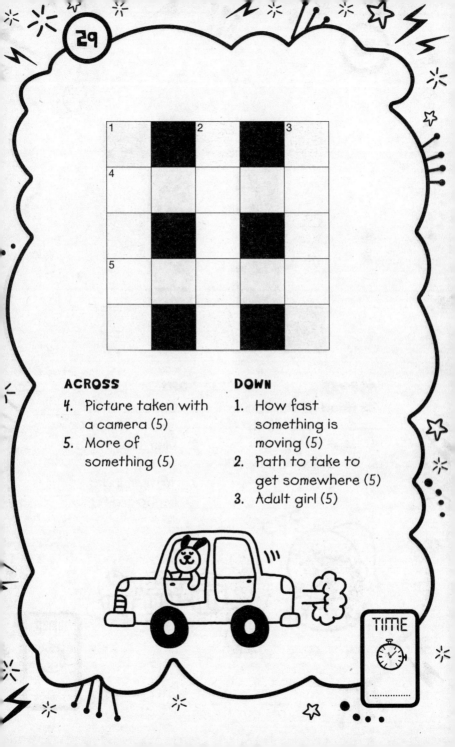

TIME

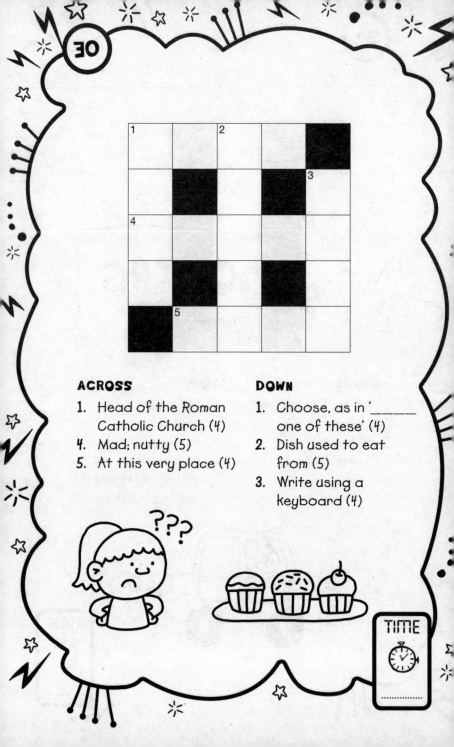

## ACROSS

1. Head of the Roman Catholic Church (4)
4. Mad; nutty (5)
5. At this very place (4)

## DOWN

1. Choose, as in '_____ one of these' (4)
2. Dish used to eat from (5)
3. Write using a keyboard (4)

???

TIME

..................

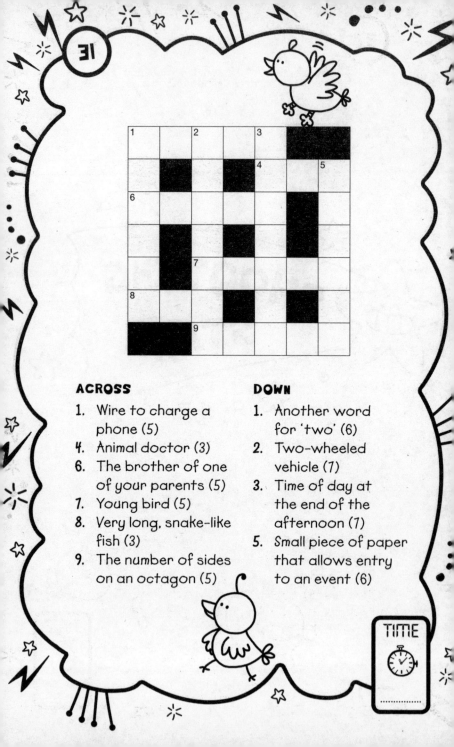

## ACROSS

1. Wire to charge a phone (5)
4. Animal doctor (3)
6. The brother of one of your parents (5)
7. Young bird (5)
8. Very long, snake-like fish (3)
9. The number of sides on an octagon (5)

## DOWN

1. Another word for 'two' (6)
2. Two-wheeled vehicle (7)
3. Time of day at the end of the afternoon (7)
5. Small piece of paper that allows entry to an event (6)

TIME

## ACROSS

1. Normal; not out of the ordinary (5)
5. Criminal who has been found guilty (7)
6. A brave or experienced fighter in battle (7)
7. Furry Australian animal that eats eucalyptus leaves (5)

## DOWN

2. More than a few (7)
3. Heavy object dropped from a boat to keep it from floating away (6)
4. Fruit used to make ketchup (6)

TIME

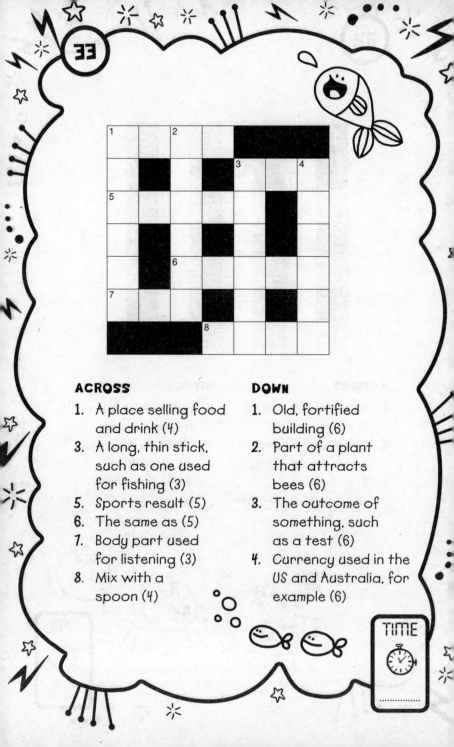

**ACROSS**

1. A place selling food and drink (4)
3. A long, thin stick, such as one used for fishing (3)
5. Sports result (5)
6. The same as (5)
7. Body part used for listening (3)
8. Mix with a spoon (4)

**DOWN**

1. Old, fortified building (6)
2. Part of a plant that attracts bees (6)
3. The outcome of something, such as a test (6)
4. Currency used in the US and Australia, for example (6)

TIME

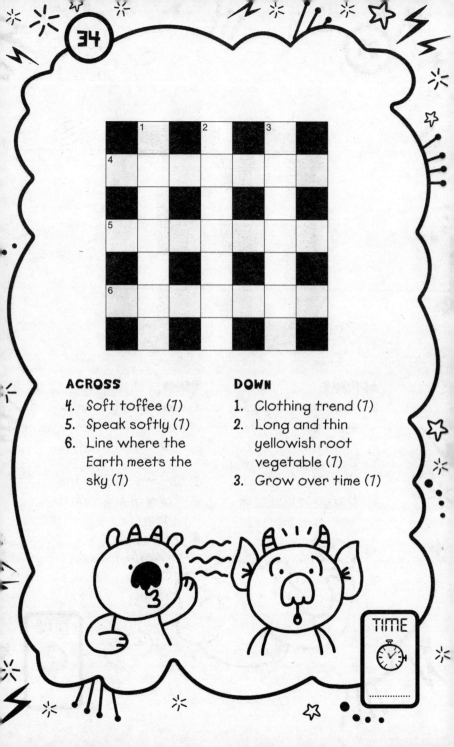

## ACROSS

4. Soft toffee (7)
5. Speak softly (7)
6. Line where the Earth meets the sky (7)

## DOWN

1. Clothing trend (7)
2. Long and thin yellowish root vegetable (7)
3. Grow over time (7)

TIME

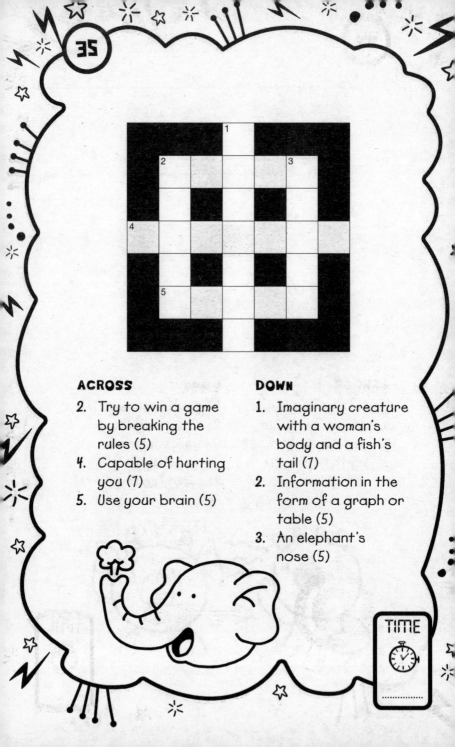

## ACROSS

2. Try to win a game by breaking the rules (5)
4. Capable of hurting you (7)
5. Use your brain (5)

## DOWN

1. Imaginary creature with a woman's body and a fish's tail (7)
2. Information in the form of a graph or table (5)
3. An elephant's nose (5)

TIME

..................

## ACROSS

1. You might use this to take photos (6)
5. A male sibling (7)
6. Not allow to be seen (7)
8. Something to aim for (6)

## DOWN

2. Place where planes take off and land (7)
3. Chew food and swallow (3)
4. Not out of the ordinary in any way (7)
7. Common road vehicle (3)

TIME

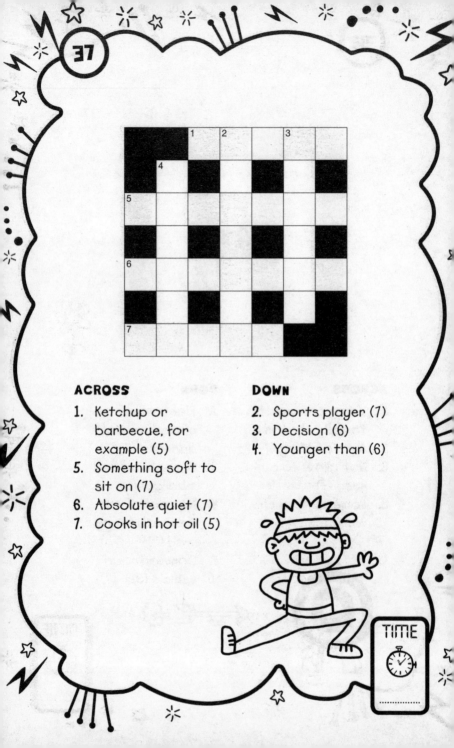

## ACROSS

1. Ketchup or barbecue, for example (5)
5. Something soft to sit on (7)
6. Absolute quiet (7)
7. Cooks in hot oil (5)

## DOWN

2. Sports player (7)
3. Decision (6)
4. Younger than (6)

TIME

## ACROSS

3. Stringed instrument played with fingers or a pick (6)
4. Period of fighting between armies (3)
5. A king or queen, perhaps (5)
7. Obtained (3)
8. Someone in charge of a group (6)

## DOWN

1. Currency used in many European countries (4)
2. Member of a ship's crew (6)
3. Outdoor recreation area, with plants and trees (6)
6. Gets older (4)

TIME

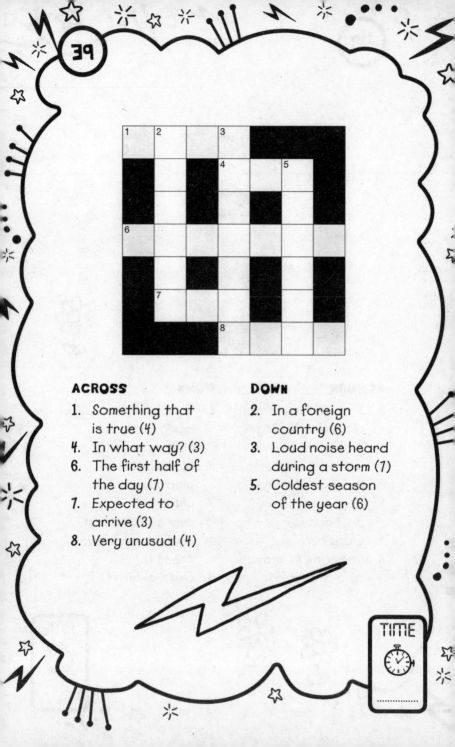

## ACROSS

1. Something that is true (4)
4. In what way? (3)
6. The first half of the day (7)
7. Expected to arrive (3)
8. Very unusual (4)

## DOWN

2. In a foreign country (6)
3. Loud noise heard during a storm (7)
5. Coldest season of the year (6)

TIME

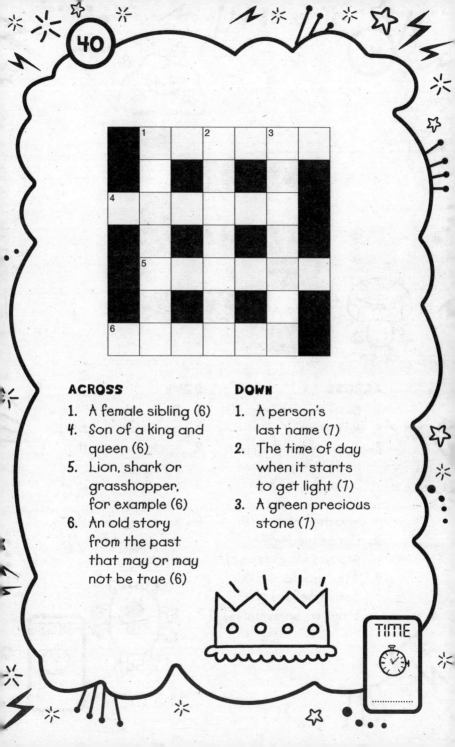

## ACROSS

1. A female sibling (6)
4. Son of a king and queen (6)
5. Lion, shark or grasshopper, for example (6)
6. An old story from the past that may or may not be true (6)

## DOWN

1. A person's last name (7)
2. The time of day when it starts to get light (7)
3. A green precious stone (7)

TIME

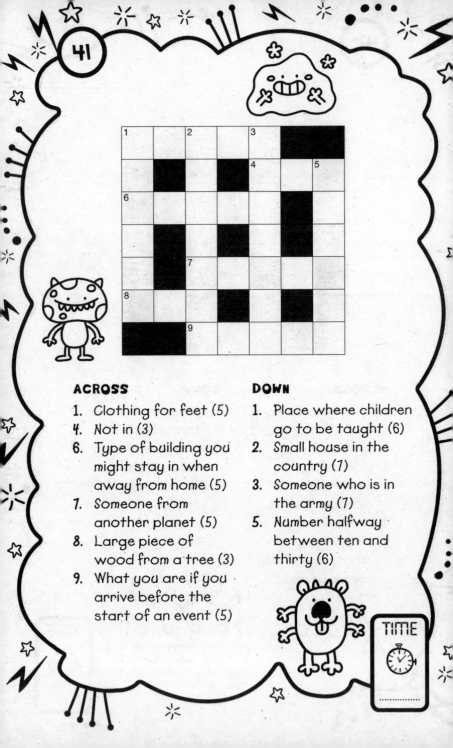

## ACROSS

1. Clothing for feet (5)
4. Not in (3)
6. Type of building you might stay in when away from home (5)
7. Someone from another planet (5)
8. Large piece of wood from a tree (3)
9. What you are if you arrive before the start of an event (5)

## DOWN

1. Place where children go to be taught (6)
2. Small house in the country (7)
3. Someone who is in the army (7)
5. Number halfway between ten and thirty (6)

TIME

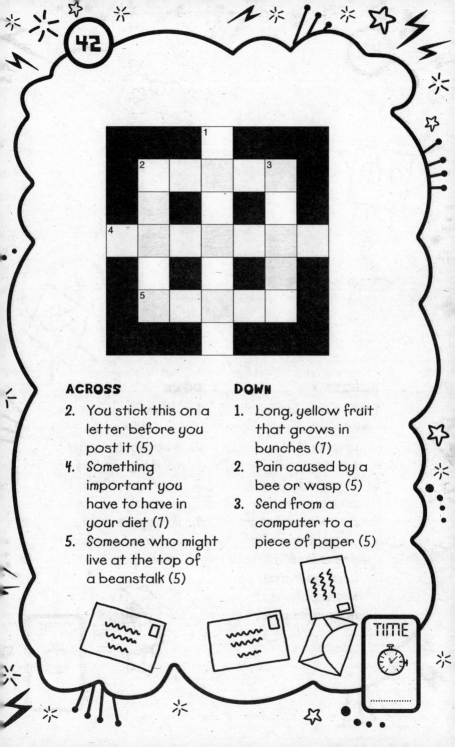

## ACROSS

2. You stick this on a letter before you post it (5)
4. Something important you have to have in your diet (7)
5. Someone who might live at the top of a beanstalk (5)

## DOWN

1. Long, yellow fruit that grows in bunches (7)
2. Pain caused by a bee or wasp (5)
3. Send from a computer to a piece of paper (5)

TIME

..............

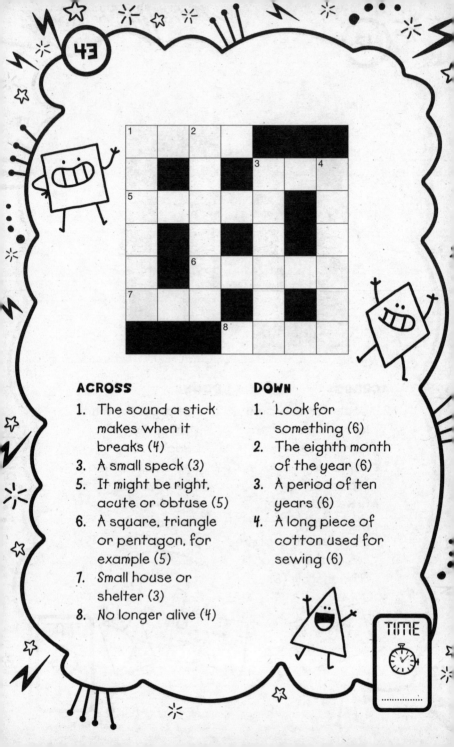

## ACROSS

1. The sound a stick makes when it breaks (4)
3. A small speck (3)
5. It might be right, acute or obtuse (5)
6. A square, triangle or pentagon, for example (5)
7. Small house or shelter (3)
8. No longer alive (4)

## DOWN

1. Look for something (6)
2. The eighth month of the year (6)
3. A period of ten years (6)
4. A long piece of cotton used for sewing (6)

TIME

.................

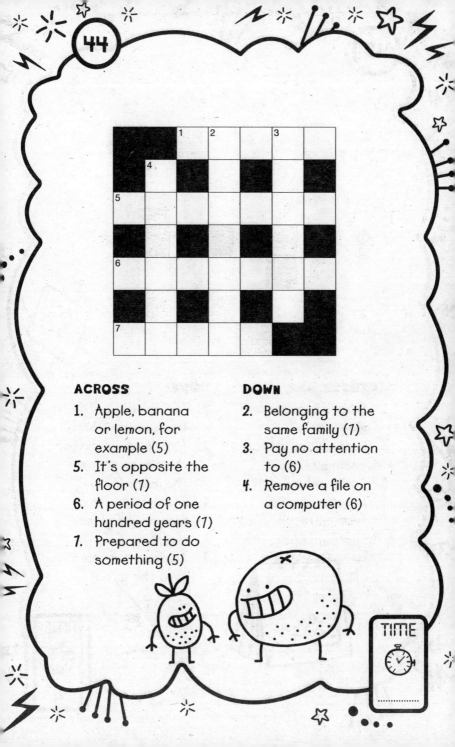

## ACROSS

1. Apple, banana or lemon, for example (5)
5. It's opposite the floor (7)
6. A period of one hundred years (7)
7. Prepared to do something (5)

## DOWN

2. Belonging to the same family (7)
3. Pay no attention to (6)
4. Remove a file on a computer (6)

TIME

## ACROSS

1. Sloped playground rides (6)
5. Hide; prevent from seeing (7)
6. Badly behaved (7)
8. Leave; go away from (6)

## DOWN

2. African big cat with a spotted coat (7)
3. An abbreviation for the final month of the year (3)
4. Break into lots of pieces, like glass might do (7)
7. A space between two things (3)

TIME

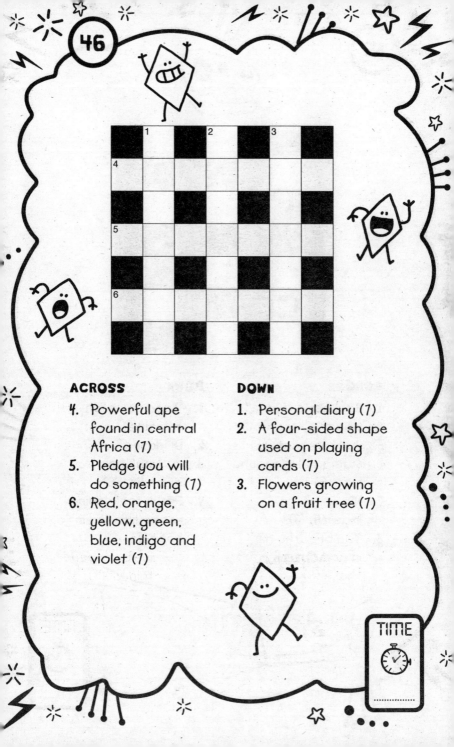

## ACROSS

4. Powerful ape found in central Africa (7)
5. Pledge you will do something (7)
6. Red, orange, yellow, green, blue, indigo and violet (7)

## DOWN

1. Personal diary (7)
2. A four-sided shape used on playing cards (7)
3. Flowers growing on a fruit tree (7)

TIME

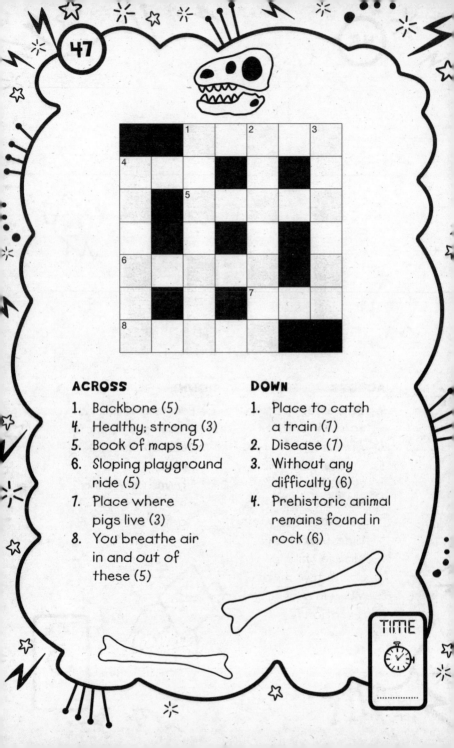

## ACROSS

1. Backbone (5)
4. Healthy; strong (3)
5. Book of maps (5)
6. Sloping playground ride (5)
7. Place where pigs live (3)
8. You breathe air in and out of these (5)

## DOWN

1. Place to catch a train (7)
2. Disease (7)
3. Without any difficulty (6)
4. Prehistoric animal remains found in rock (6)

TIME

..............

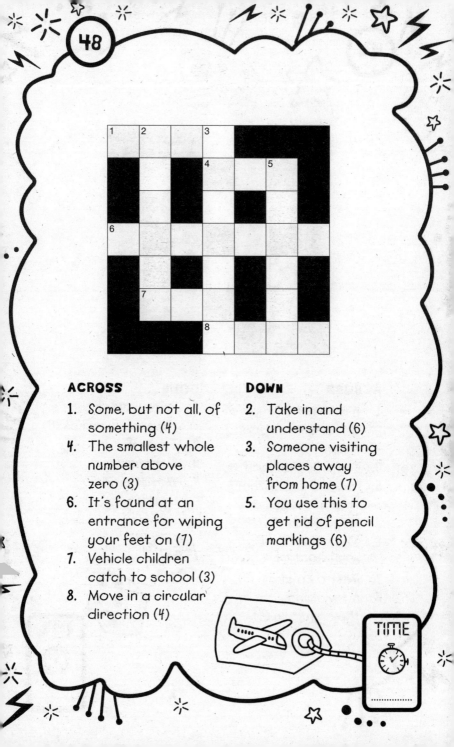

## ACROSS

1. Some, but not all, of something (4)
4. The smallest whole number above zero (3)
6. It's found at an entrance for wiping your feet on (7)
7. Vehicle children catch to school (3)
8. Move in a circular direction (4)

## DOWN

2. Take in and understand (6)
3. Someone visiting places away from home (7)
5. You use this to get rid of pencil markings (6)

TIME

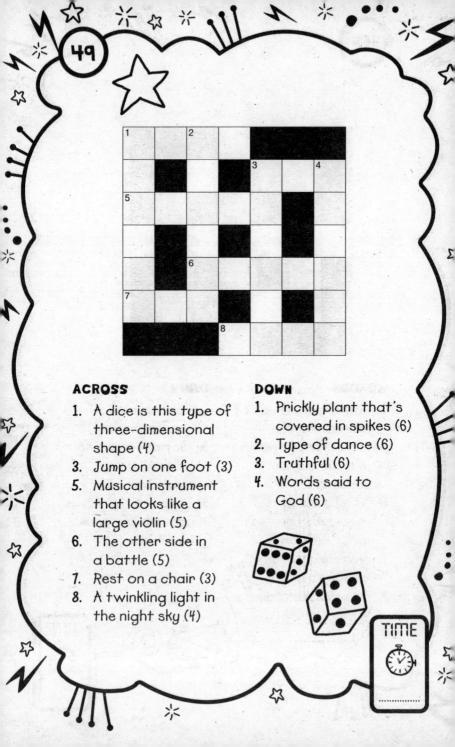

## ACROSS

1. A dice is this type of three-dimensional shape (4)
3. Jump on one foot (3)
5. Musical instrument that looks like a large violin (5)
6. The other side in a battle (5)
7. Rest on a chair (3)
8. A twinkling light in the night sky (4)

## DOWN

1. Prickly plant that's covered in spikes (6)
2. Type of dance (6)
3. Truthful (6)
4. Words said to God (6)

TIME

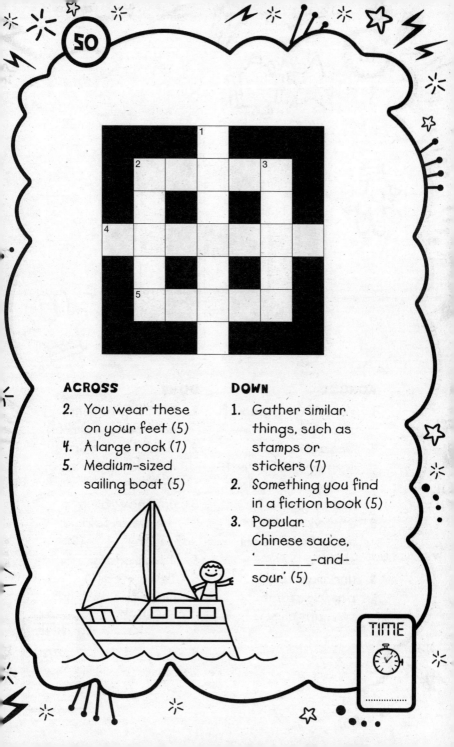

## ACROSS

2. You wear these on your feet (5)
4. A large rock (7)
5. Medium-sized sailing boat (5)

## DOWN

1. Gather similar things, such as stamps or stickers (7)
2. Something you find in a fiction book (5)
3. Popular Chinese sauce, '_____-and-sour' (5)

TIME
............

## ACROSS

1. Very large group of stars (6)
4. Grass and leaves that are left to rot, then used to help plants grow (7)
6. Strong material made from animal skin (7)
8. Underground passage (6)

## DOWN

1. Clothing to keep your hand warm (5)
2. Fleshy area above or below the mouth opening (3)
3. Until now, as in 'I haven't told anyone _____' (3)
5. Take illegally (5)
6. Illuminated (3)
7. One more than nine (3)

TIME

........................

## ACROSS

3. Place where criminals are confined (6)
4. Say something that isn't true (3)
5. React to a joke, perhaps (5)
7. Part of the body between the feet and the hips (3)
8. Someone who steals things (6)

## DOWN

1. A measurement that's equal to width times length for a rectangle (4)
2. A female parent (6)
3. Cushion for sleeping on (6)
6. Great delight (4)

TIME

..................

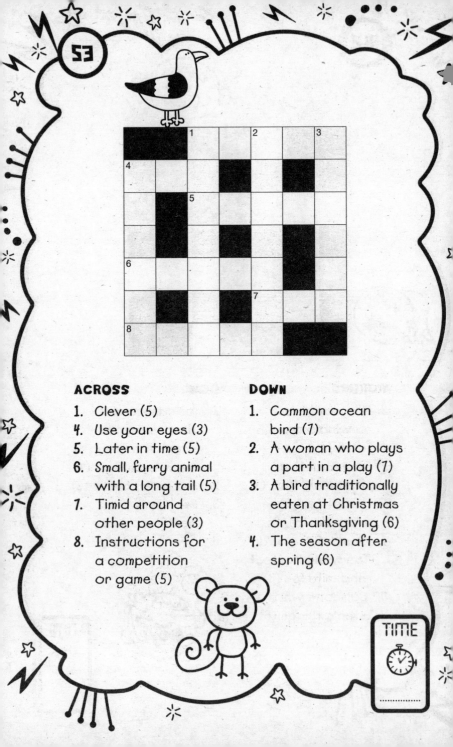

## ACROSS

1. Clever (5)
4. Use your eyes (3)
5. Later in time (5)
6. Small, furry animal with a long tail (5)
7. Timid around other people (3)
8. Instructions for a competition or game (5)

## DOWN

1. Common ocean bird (7)
2. A woman who plays a part in a play (7)
3. A bird traditionally eaten at Christmas or Thanksgiving (6)
4. The season after spring (6)

TIME

.............

## ACROSS

1. You do this to show that you're happy (5)
5. Final course of a meal (7)
6. Something you might do to stop an itch (7)
7. The sharp part of a knife (5)

## DOWN

2. Hot-tasting yellow sauce, sometimes eaten with ham (7)
3. The words of a song (6)
4. Erasable writing tool (6)

TIME

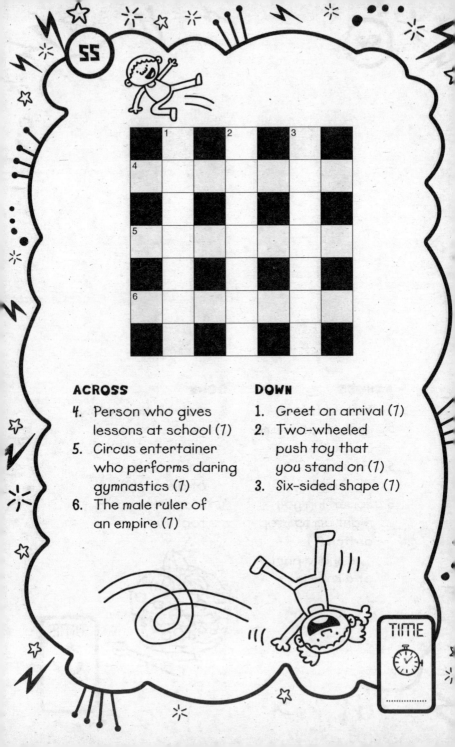

## ACROSS

4. Person who gives lessons at school (7)
5. Circus entertainer who performs daring gymnastics (7)
6. The male ruler of an empire (7)

## DOWN

1. Greet on arrival (7)
2. Two-wheeled push toy that you stand on (7)
3. Six-sided shape (7)

TIME

## ACROSS

1. Got older (4)
4. Small creature that helps Santa (3)
6. A strong feeling (7)
7. The opposite of no (3)
8. Really small (4)

## DOWN

2. Bad-tempered (6)
3. A person whose job it is to treat teeth (7)
5. Made of solid water (6)

TIME

## ACROSS

1. The opposite of narrow (4)
3. A group of related items (3)
5. What the sun provides for us (5)
6. 'New line' key on a keyboard (5)
7. Fasten, as in '____ your shoelaces' (3)
8. A home a bird might build (4)

## DOWN

1. Edible nut with a wrinkly surface (6)
2. Unit used for measuring angles (6)
3. Large, sculpted model of a person or animal (6)
4. Desire for a drink (6)

TIME

......................

## ACROSS

1. Road (6)
4. Marriage ceremony (7)
6. Details of where someone lives (7)
8. Decorative cup awarded as a prize (6)

## DOWN

1. Use money to buy something (5)
2. Tool used for fishing (3)
3. Label attached to a present (3)
5. Not very nice (5)
6. Drawings, paintings or sculptures (3)
7. Tear something, such as a piece of paper (3)

TIME

**59**

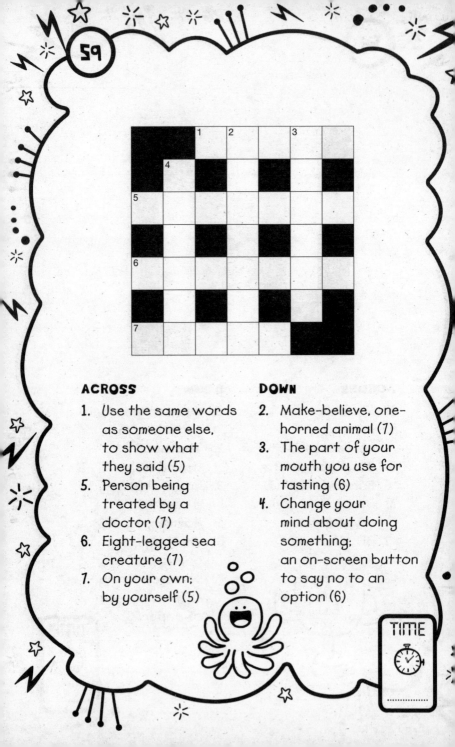

## ACROSS

1. Use the same words as someone else, to show what they said (5)
5. Person being treated by a doctor (7)
6. Eight-legged sea creature (7)
7. On your own; by yourself (5)

## DOWN

2. Make-believe, one-horned animal (7)
3. The part of your mouth you use for tasting (6)
4. Change your mind about doing something; an on-screen button to say no to an option (6)

TIME

## ACROSS

3. Travel behind someone else (6)
4. Paddle used to row a boat (3)
5. Fierce weather event with thunder and lightning (5)
7. Tree on which acorns grow (3)
8. Tell a secret, for example (6)

## DOWN

1. Defensive building with strong walls (4)
2. Usual; ordinary (6)
3. At a greater speed (6)
6. You drive a vehicle on this (4)

TIME

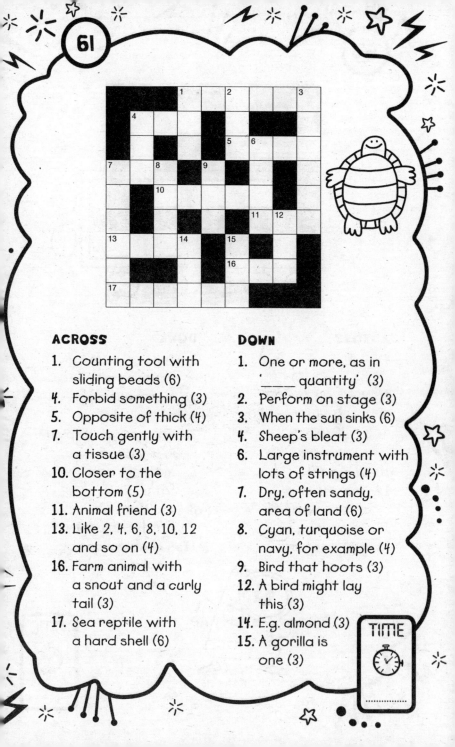

## ACROSS

1. Counting tool with sliding beads (6)
4. Forbid something (3)
5. Opposite of thick (4)
7. Touch gently with a tissue (3)
10. Closer to the bottom (5)
11. Animal friend (3)
13. Like 2, 4, 6, 8, 10, 12 and so on (4)
16. Farm animal with a snout and a curly tail (3)
17. Sea reptile with a hard shell (6)

## DOWN

1. One or more, as in '_____ quantity' (3)
2. Perform on stage (3)
3. When the sun sinks (6)
4. Sheep's bleat (3)
6. Large instrument with lots of strings (4)
7. Dry, often sandy, area of land (6)
8. Cyan, turquoise or navy, for example (4)
9. Bird that hoots (3)
12. A bird might lay this (3)
14. E.g. almond (3)
15. A gorilla is one (3)

TIME

..................

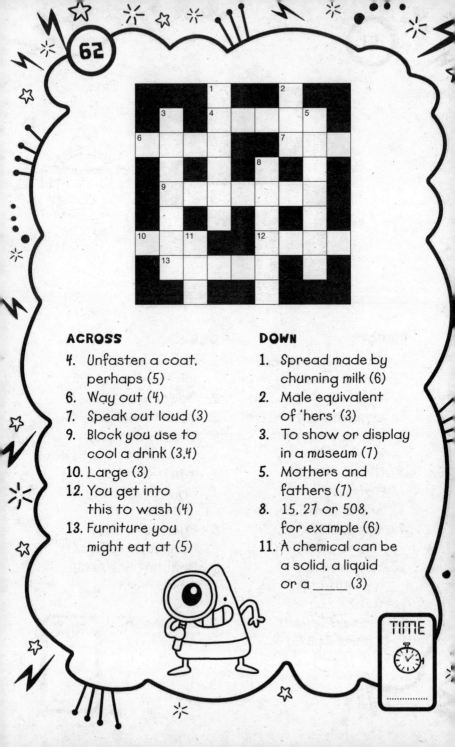

## ACROSS

4. Unfasten a coat, perhaps (5)
6. Way out (4)
7. Speak out loud (3)
9. Block you use to cool a drink (3,4)
10. Large (3)
12. You get into this to wash (4)
13. Furniture you might eat at (5)

## DOWN

1. Spread made by churning milk (6)
2. Male equivalent of 'hers' (3)
3. To show or display in a museum (7)
5. Mothers and fathers (7)
8. 15, 27 or 508, for example (6)
11. A chemical can be a solid, a liquid or a _____ (3)

TIME

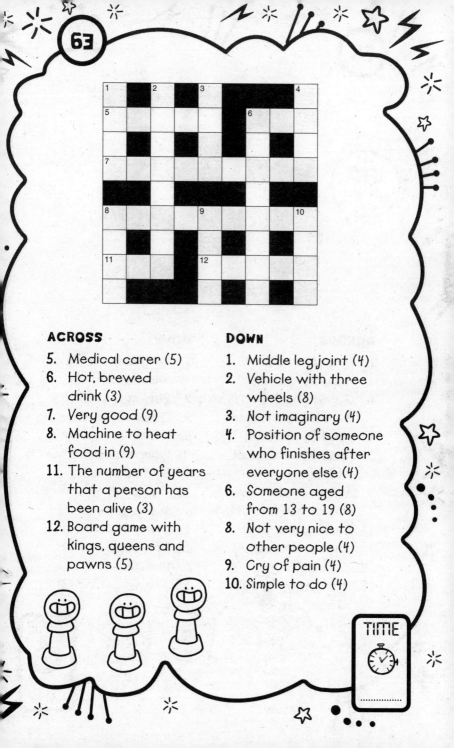

## ACROSS

5. Medical carer (5)
6. Hot, brewed drink (3)
7. Very good (9)
8. Machine to heat food in (9)
11. The number of years that a person has been alive (3)
12. Board game with kings, queens and pawns (5)

## DOWN

1. Middle leg joint (4)
2. Vehicle with three wheels (8)
3. Not imaginary (4)
4. Position of someone who finishes after everyone else (4)
6. Someone aged from 13 to 19 (8)
8. Not very nice to other people (4)
9. Cry of pain (4)
10. Simple to do (4)

TIME

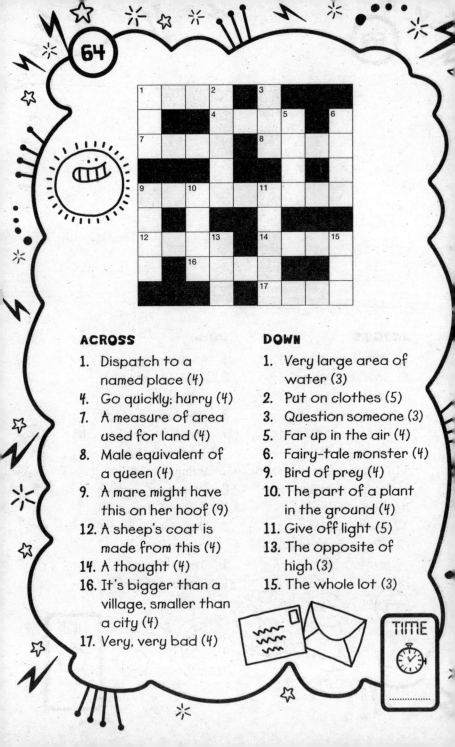

## ACROSS

1. Dispatch to a named place (4)
4. Go quickly; hurry (4)
7. A measure of area used for land (4)
8. Male equivalent of a queen (4)
9. A mare might have this on her hoof (9)
12. A sheep's coat is made from this (4)
14. A thought (4)
16. It's bigger than a village, smaller than a city (4)
17. Very, very bad (4)

## DOWN

1. Very large area of water (3)
2. Put on clothes (5)
3. Question someone (3)
5. Far up in the air (4)
6. Fairy-tale monster (4)
9. Bird of prey (4)
10. The part of a plant in the ground (4)
11. Give off light (5)
13. The opposite of high (3)
15. The whole lot (3)

TIME

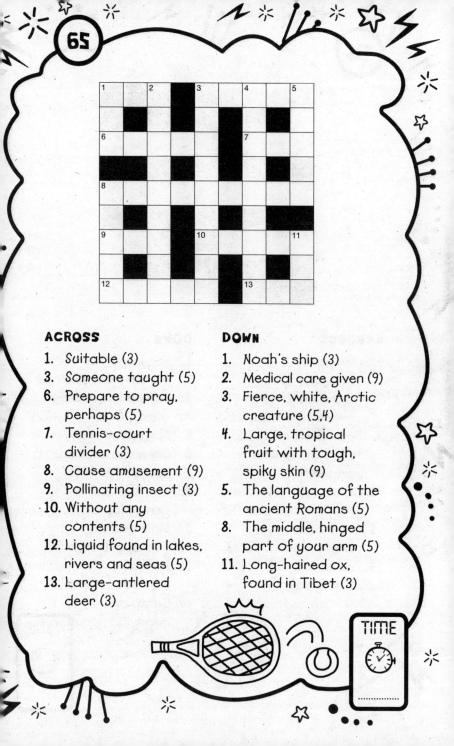

## ACROSS

1. Suitable (3)
3. Someone taught (5)
6. Prepare to pray, perhaps (5)
7. Tennis-court divider (3)
8. Cause amusement (9)
9. Pollinating insect (3)
10. Without any contents (5)
12. Liquid found in lakes, rivers and seas (5)
13. Large-antlered deer (3)

## DOWN

1. Noah's ship (3)
2. Medical care given (9)
3. Fierce, white, Arctic creature (5,4)
4. Large, tropical fruit with tough, spiky skin (9)
5. The language of the ancient Romans (5)
8. The middle, hinged part of your arm (5)
11. Long-haired ox, found in Tibet (3)

TIME

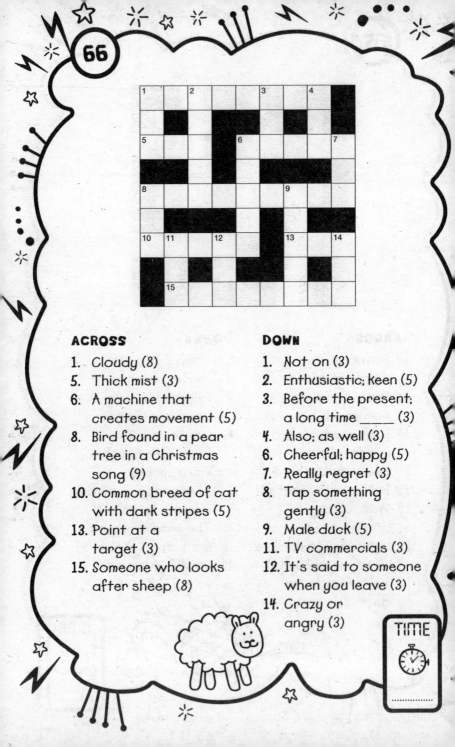

## ACROSS

1. Cloudy (8)
5. Thick mist (3)
6. A machine that creates movement (5)
8. Bird found in a pear tree in a Christmas song (9)
10. Common breed of cat with dark stripes (5)
13. Point at a target (3)
15. Someone who looks after sheep (8)

## DOWN

1. Not on (3)
2. Enthusiastic; keen (5)
3. Before the present; a long time _____ (3)
4. Also; as well (3)
6. Cheerful; happy (5)
7. Really regret (3)
8. Tap something gently (3)
9. Male duck (5)
11. TV commercials (3)
12. It's said to someone when you leave (3)
14. Crazy or angry (3)

TIME

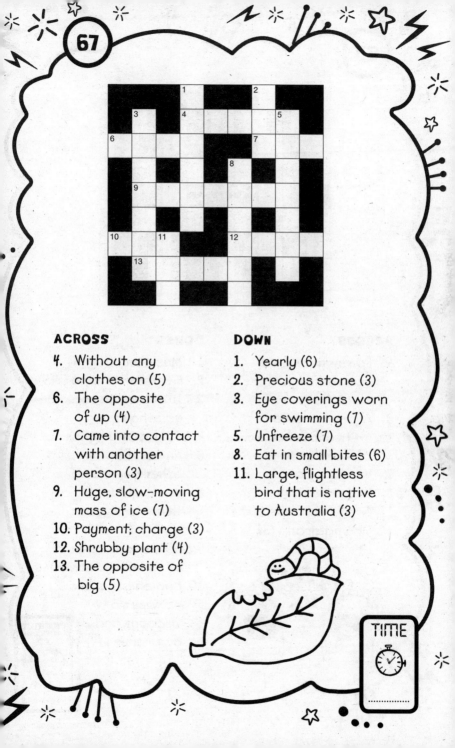

## ACROSS

4. Without any clothes on (5)
6. The opposite of up (4)
7. Came into contact with another person (3)
9. Huge, slow-moving mass of ice (7)
10. Payment; charge (3)
12. Shrubby plant (4)
13. The opposite of big (5)

## DOWN

1. Yearly (6)
2. Precious stone (3)
3. Eye coverings worn for swimming (7)
5. Unfreeze (7)
8. Eat in small bites (6)
11. Large, flightless bird that is native to Australia (3)

TIME

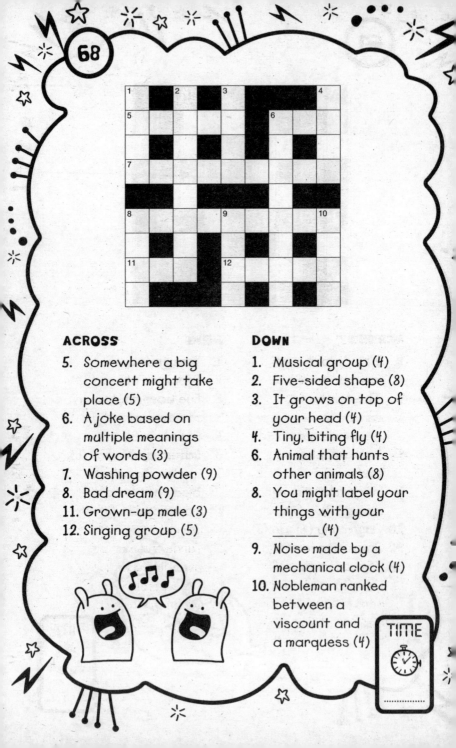

## ACROSS

5. Somewhere a big concert might take place (5)
6. A joke based on multiple meanings of words (3)
7. Washing powder (9)
8. Bad dream (9)
11. Grown-up male (3)
12. Singing group (5)

## DOWN

1. Musical group (4)
2. Five-sided shape (8)
3. It grows on top of your head (4)
4. Tiny, biting fly (4)
6. Animal that hunts other animals (8)
8. You might label your things with your _____ (4)
9. Noise made by a mechanical clock (4)
10. Nobleman ranked between a viscount and a marquess (4)

TIME

## ACROSS

1. A story of heroic adventure (4)
4. Depend (4)
7. List of food options in a restaurant (4)
8. Give out playing cards (4)
9. Mark left by a step (9)
12. Very many (4)
14. Good chance (4)
16. Loose earth (4)
17. It's often placed next to pepper on a dinner table (4)

## DOWN

1. Tree that's an anagram of 'Mel' (3)
2. The browned edge of a loaf of bread (5)
3. Not new (3)
5. Fabled ape-man of the Himalayas (4)
6. Story of a movie (4)
9. A saved document (4)
10. Porridge cereal (4)
11. Turns over and over, like a ball (5)
13. Male offspring (3)
15. Set of parts to build a model (3)

TIME

..............

## ACROSS

1. Cured pig's meat (3)
3. You shed these when you cry (5)
6. Device that makes a warning noise (5)
7. Thick, black liquid for road surfaces (3)
8. Figure used to keep birds off crops (9)
9. A long period (3)
10. Elephants' tusks are made of this (5)
12. Not here but _____ (5)
13. A negative word (3)

## DOWN

1. Possesses (3)
2. Sweet spread, often made with oranges (9)
3. Type of small orange (9)
4. Part of the day between morning and evening (9)
5. Long, narrow tube for drinking (5)
8. Bed covering; piece of paper (5)
11. So far (3)

TIME

..................

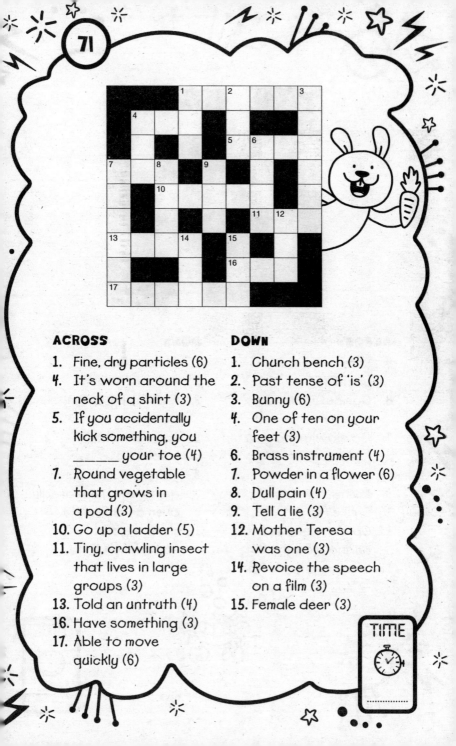

## ACROSS

1. Fine, dry particles (6)
4. It's worn around the neck of a shirt (3)
5. If you accidentally kick something, you _____ your toe (4)
7. Round vegetable that grows in a pod (3)
10. Go up a ladder (5)
11. Tiny, crawling insect that lives in large groups (3)
13. Told an untruth (4)
16. Have something (3)
17. Able to move quickly (6)

## DOWN

1. Church bench (3)
2. Past tense of 'is' (3)
3. Bunny (6)
4. One of ten on your feet (3)
6. Brass instrument (4)
7. Powder in a flower (6)
8. Dull pain (4)
9. Tell a lie (3)
12. Mother Teresa was one (3)
14. Revoice the speech on a film (3)
15. Female deer (3)

TIME

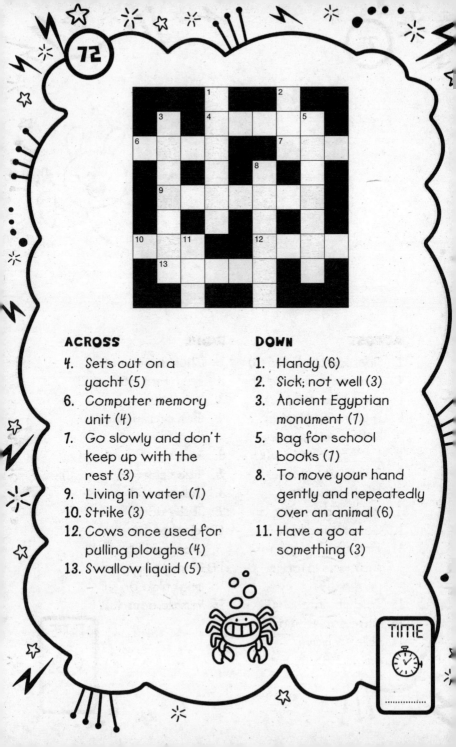

## ACROSS

4. Sets out on a yacht (5)
6. Computer memory unit (4)
7. Go slowly and don't keep up with the rest (3)
9. Living in water (7)
10. Strike (3)
12. Cows once used for pulling ploughs (4)
13. Swallow liquid (5)

## DOWN

1. Handy (6)
2. Sick; not well (3)
3. Ancient Egyptian monument (7)
5. Bag for school books (7)
8. To move your hand gently and repeatedly over an animal (6)
11. Have a go at something (3)

TIME

.................

## ACROSS

5. Remove all traces (5)
6. A material that is mined for the metal or minerals in it (3)
7. Soft, cuddly toy (5,4)
8. Expert at a university (9)
11. Had a meal (3)
12. A prize given for an achievement (5)

## DOWN

1. Grated peel of a lemon or orange (4)
2. Cupboard for hanging clothes (8)
3. Extremely, as in 'she was _____ old' (4)
4. Back part (4)
6. Abroad (8)
8. Take part in a game (4)
9. Academic test (4)
10. Something you might go on at a theme park (4)

TIME

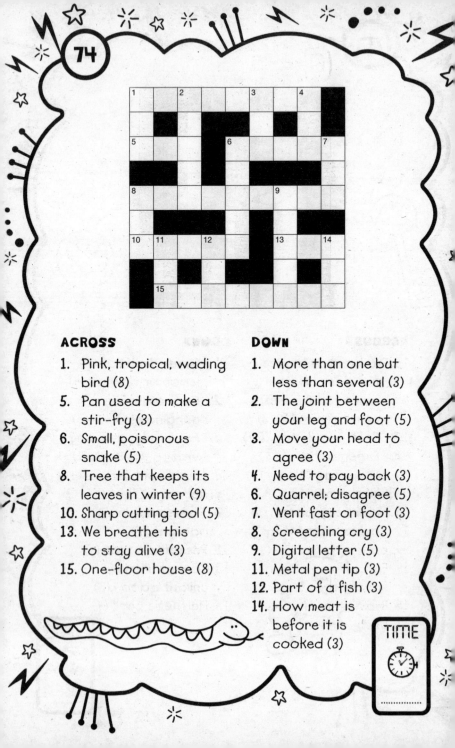

## ACROSS

1. Pink, tropical, wading bird (8)
5. Pan used to make a stir-fry (3)
6. Small, poisonous snake (5)
8. Tree that keeps its leaves in winter (9)
10. Sharp cutting tool (5)
13. We breathe this to stay alive (3)
15. One-floor house (8)

## DOWN

1. More than one but less than several (3)
2. The joint between your leg and foot (5)
3. Move your head to agree (3)
4. Need to pay back (3)
6. Quarrel; disagree (5)
7. Went fast on foot (3)
8. Screeching cry (3)
9. Digital letter (5)
11. Metal pen tip (3)
12. Part of a fish (3)
14. How meat is before it is cooked (3)

TIME

..................

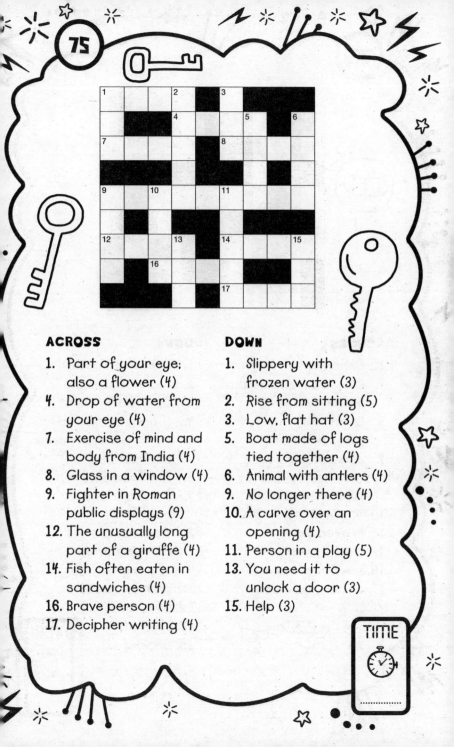

**75**

## ACROSS

1. Part of your eye; also a flower (4)
4. Drop of water from your eye (4)
7. Exercise of mind and body from India (4)
8. Glass in a window (4)
9. Fighter in Roman public displays (9)
12. The unusually long part of a giraffe (4)
14. Fish often eaten in sandwiches (4)
16. Brave person (4)
17. Decipher writing (4)

## DOWN

1. Slippery with frozen water (3)
2. Rise from sitting (5)
3. Low, flat hat (3)
5. Boat made of logs tied together (4)
6. Animal with antlers (4)
9. No longer there (4)
10. A curve over an opening (4)
11. Person in a play (5)
13. You need it to unlock a door (3)
15. Help (3)

TIME

..............

## ACROSS

1. Unhappiness (6)
4. Illness often caught in the winter (3)
5. Deep breath when you are tired (4)
7. Somewhere you can visit to see wild animals (3)
10. Man's chin hair (5)
11. Female pig (3)
13. Cow's meat (4)
16. Seed container (3)
17. Other than, as in 'I want them all, _____ for that' (6)

## DOWN

1. Take legal action (3)
2. Beam of sunlight (3)
3. Opening in a wall (6)
4. If you run to and ____, you go there and back (3)
6. Sums numbers (4)
7. A 'living' dead person (6)
8. Woodwind instrument (4)
9. You might wipe your feet on this (3)
12. Strange (3)
14. Enemy (3)
15. Choose (3)

TIME

..............

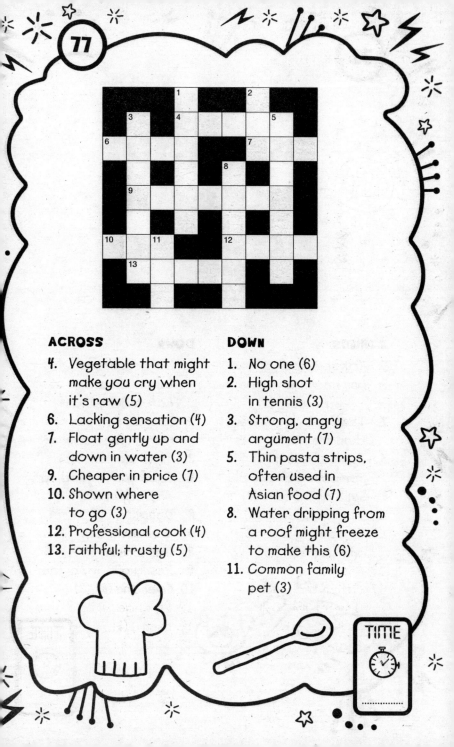

## ACROSS

4. Vegetable that might make you cry when it's raw (5)
6. Lacking sensation (4)
7. Float gently up and down in water (3)
9. Cheaper in price (7)
10. Shown where to go (3)
12. Professional cook (4)
13. Faithful; trusty (5)

## DOWN

1. No one (6)
2. High shot in tennis (3)
3. Strong, angry argument (7)
5. Thin pasta strips, often used in Asian food (7)
8. Water dripping from a roof might freeze to make this (6)
11. Common family pet (3)

TIME

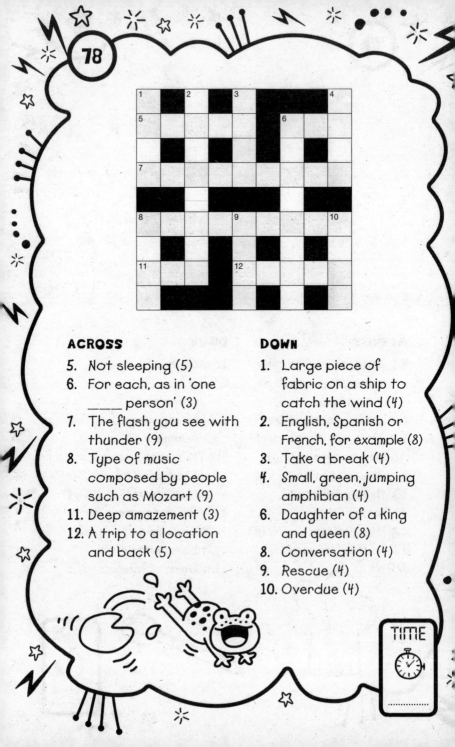

## ACROSS

5. Not sleeping (5)
6. For each, as in 'one ____ person' (3)
7. The flash you see with thunder (9)
8. Type of music composed by people such as Mozart (9)
11. Deep amazement (3)
12. A trip to a location and back (5)

## DOWN

1. Large piece of fabric on a ship to catch the wind (4)
2. English, Spanish or French, for example (8)
3. Take a break (4)
4. Small, green, jumping amphibian (4)
6. Daughter of a king and queen (8)
8. Conversation (4)
9. Rescue (4)
10. Overdue (4)

TIME

## ACROSS

1. All the letters in a language (8)
5. Loud noise (3)
6. Welsh breed of dog (5)
8. Go with (9)
10. Organ that pumps blood (5)
13. Use oars to move a boat (3)
15. Way in (8)

## DOWN

1. Sum two or more numbers (3)
2. Overwhelming fear and confusion (5)
3. Shout this to scare (3)
4. Hard pull (3)
6. It has a bright tail in the night sky (5)
7. Evergreen climber (3)
8. Remains of a fire (3)
9. It's worn to protect the front of clothes (5)
11. 24th December is Christmas ____ (3)
12. Large rodent (3)
14. Great distress (3)

TIME

## ACROSS

1. Black playing card (4)
4. A swelling (4)
7. Pleasant (4)
8. Not having very much money (4)
9. The day before today (9)
12. Device for stopping someone from opening a door (4)
14. Slightly open (4)
16. Nice to others (4)
17. Road marker that shows the way (4)

## DOWN

1. Metal container (3)
2. Sound made by a sheep or goat (5)
3. Mischievous pixie (3)
5. Small lake (4)
6. Photograph showing inside you (1-3)
9. Shout loudly (4)
10. Santa's bag (4)
11. Wide paths, for vehicles (5)
13. Small child (3)
15. Sprint (3)

TIME

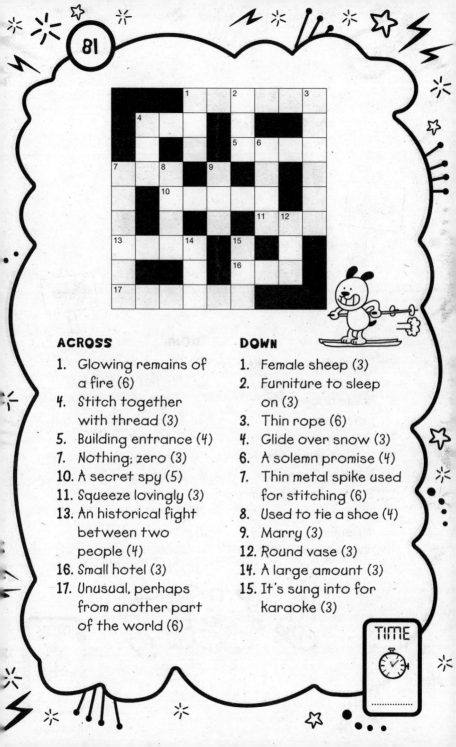

## ACROSS

1. Glowing remains of a fire (6)
4. Stitch together with thread (3)
5. Building entrance (4)
7. Nothing; zero (3)
10. A secret spy (5)
11. Squeeze lovingly (3)
13. An historical fight between two people (4)
16. Small hotel (3)
17. Unusual, perhaps from another part of the world (6)

## DOWN

1. Female sheep (3)
2. Furniture to sleep on (3)
3. Thin rope (6)
4. Glide over snow (3)
6. A solemn promise (4)
7. Thin metal spike used for stitching (6)
8. Used to tie a shoe (4)
9. Marry (3)
12. Round vase (3)
14. A large amount (3)
15. It's sung into for karaoke (3)

TIME

## ACROSS

4. Someone who makes and sells bread (5)
6. Feline household pets (4)
7. Grown-up boys (3)
9. Violent windstorm (7)
10. A type of pig (3)
12. Strong emotion of liking someone very much (4)
13. Non-musical sound (5)

## DOWN

1. Silly; ridiculous (6)
2. Folded and sewn edge of cloth (3)
3. Give a warning (7)
5. Turn around in a circle (7)
8. Carry case for money and cards (6)
11. Deity; a being that is worshipped (3)

TIME

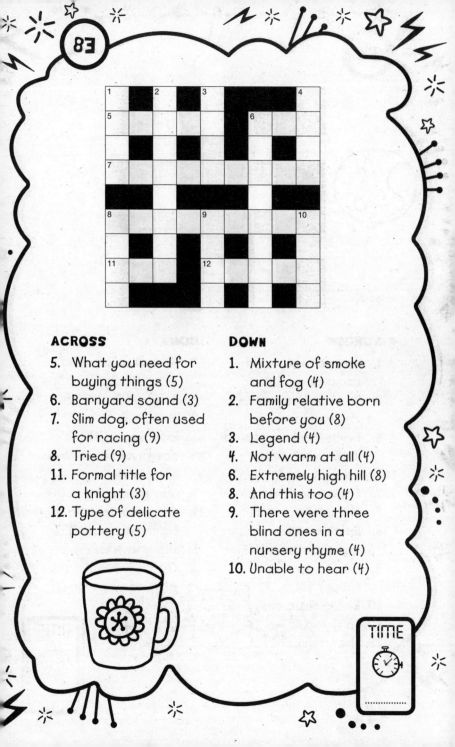

## ACROSS

5. What you need for buying things (5)
6. Barnyard sound (3)
7. Slim dog, often used for racing (9)
8. Tried (9)
11. Formal title for a knight (3)
12. Type of delicate pottery (5)

## DOWN

1. Mixture of smoke and fog (4)
2. Family relative born before you (8)
3. Legend (4)
4. Not warm at all (4)
6. Extremely high hill (8)
8. And this too (4)
9. There were three blind ones in a nursery rhyme (4)
10. Unable to hear (4)

TIME

# 84

## ACROSS

1. An informal word for a medic (3)
3. Book with maps of the world in (5)
6. Long-necked musical instrument with strings to pluck (5)
7. Sound made by a sheep (3)
8. Software for a PS4, Xbox or Switch (5,4)
9. Health and beauty resort (3)
10. Really silly person (5)
12. Sampling (5)
13. Short sleep (3)

## DOWN

1. Touch gently and repeatedly, perhaps to dry (3)
2. People from a country to the north of the United States (9)
3. Say sorry (9)
4. Someone to help you borrow books (9)
5. Digging tool (5)
8. Go to see, such as a person or place (5)
11. The highest part of something (3)

TIME

## ACROSS

1. Total; complete (8)
5. A part of your body used to see (3)
6. The opposite of goodbye (5)
8. Wall decoration in rolls (9)
10. Unpleasant to listen to (5)
13. One or more of something (3)
15. Birds' wings are covered with these (8)

## DOWN

1. Gorilla or chimp (3)
2. A witch might cast this (5)
3. Operate (3)
4. Snake-shaped fish (3)
6. How you usually feel when smiling (5)
7. Piece of wood used for rowing (3)
8. Was first in a race (3)
9. Time without war (5)
11. Gone bad, like milk (3)
12. Large area of salt water (3)
14. Opposite of no (3)

TIME

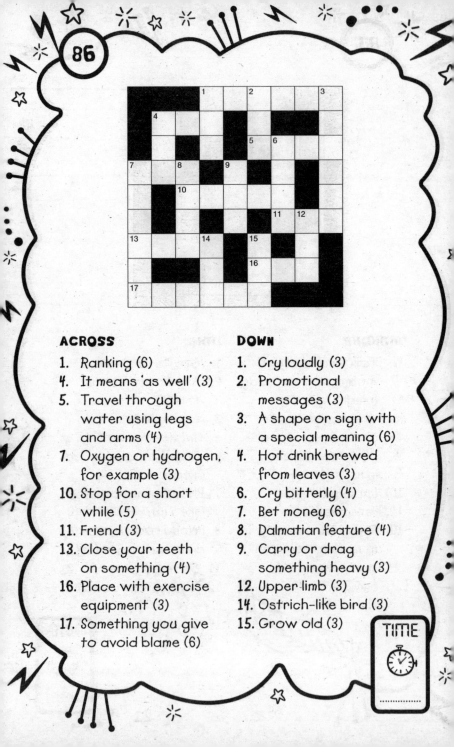

## ACROSS

1. Ranking (6)
4. It means 'as well' (3)
5. Travel through water using legs and arms (4)
7. Oxygen or hydrogen, for example (3)
10. Stop for a short while (5)
11. Friend (3)
13. Close your teeth on something (4)
16. Place with exercise equipment (3)
17. Something you give to avoid blame (6)

## DOWN

1. Cry loudly (3)
2. Promotional messages (3)
3. A shape or sign with a special meaning (6)
4. Hot drink brewed from leaves (3)
6. Cry bitterly (4)
7. Bet money (6)
8. Dalmatian feature (4)
9. Carry or drag something heavy (3)
12. Upper limb (3)
14. Ostrich-like bird (3)
15. Grow old (3)

TIME

...............

## ACROSS

4. Book for collecting photos or stamps (5)
6. Number of sides a rectangle has (4)
7. Steal (3)
9. Strapped shoes worn in summer (7)
10. Not dry (3)
12. Long walk (4)
13. Device that can pick up music or speech transmissions (5)

## DOWN

1. Mother or father (6)
2. Soft covering on an animal (3)
3. Edible shellfish with two large claws (7)
5. Frightening creature (7)
8. Picture permanently inked into the skin (6)
11. Briefly touch, as on a phone screen (3)

TIME

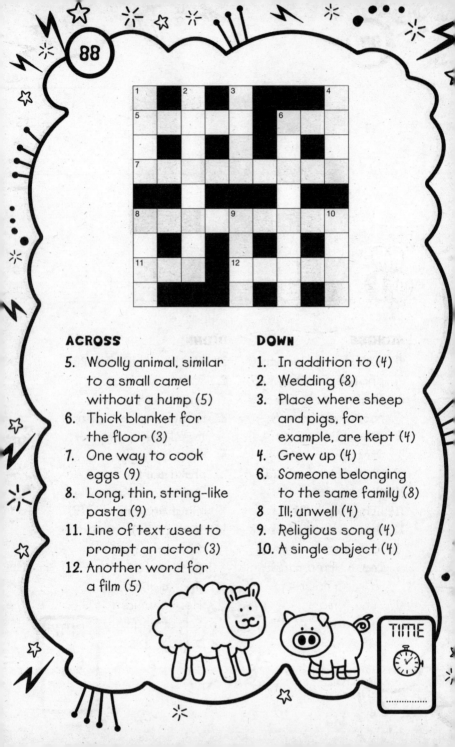

## ACROSS

5. Woolly animal, similar to a small camel without a hump (5)
6. Thick blanket for the floor (3)
7. One way to cook eggs (9)
8. Long, thin, string-like pasta (9)
11. Line of text used to prompt an actor (3)
12. Another word for a film (5)

## DOWN

1. In addition to (4)
2. Wedding (8)
3. Place where sheep and pigs, for example, are kept (4)
4. Grew up (4)
6. Someone belonging to the same family (8)
8. Ill; unwell (4)
9. Religious song (4)
10. A single object (4)

TIME

## ACROSS

1. Slope to drive up (4)
4. Twelve of these units make a foot (4)
7. A bee might do this (4)
8. Creature similar to a frog (4)
9. Struggling to wait (9)
12. Price (4)
14. The opposite of entrance (4)
16. Comfortable, long seat often found in a living room (4)
17. The female equivalent of 'gentleman' (4)

## DOWN

1. What Aladdin had to do to the lamp to summon the genie (3)
2. Baked dough topped with cheese, tomato and other foods (5)
3. Take part in a play (3)
5. A gap or pit (4)
6. Change some writing (4)
9. Scratch (4)
10. Succeed at a test (4)
11. Just right (5)
13. Heavy weight (3)
15. Something for a child to play with (3)

TIME

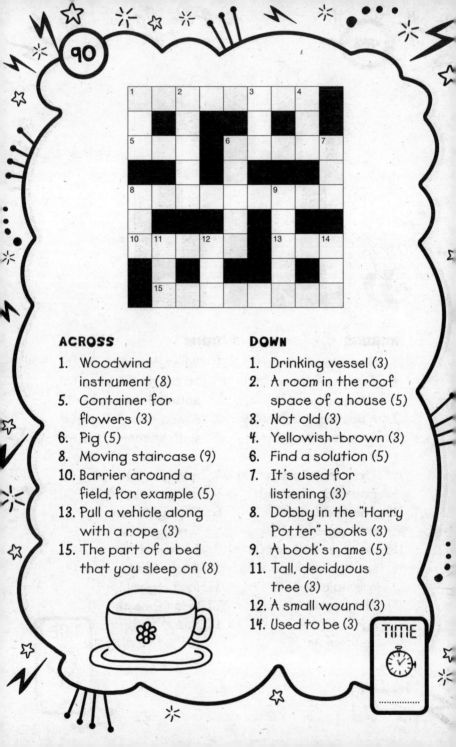

## ACROSS

1. Woodwind instrument (8)
5. Container for flowers (3)
6. Pig (5)
8. Moving staircase (9)
10. Barrier around a field, for example (5)
13. Pull a vehicle along with a rope (3)
15. The part of a bed that you sleep on (8)

## DOWN

1. Drinking vessel (3)
2. A room in the roof space of a house (5)
3. Not old (3)
4. Yellowish-brown (3)
6. Find a solution (5)
7. It's used for listening (3)
8. Dobby in the "Harry Potter" books (3)
9. A book's name (5)
11. Tall, deciduous tree (3)
12. A small wound (3)
14. Used to be (3)

TIME

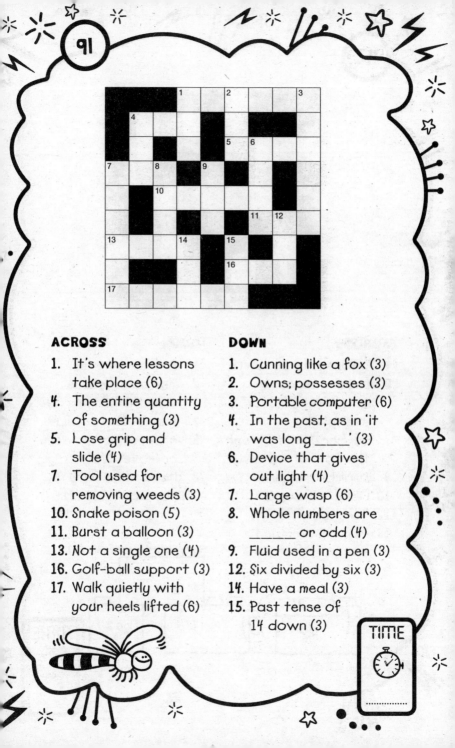

## ACROSS

1. It's where lessons take place (6)
4. The entire quantity of something (3)
5. Lose grip and slide (4)
7. Tool used for removing weeds (3)
10. Snake poison (5)
11. Burst a balloon (3)
13. Not a single one (4)
16. Golf-ball support (3)
17. Walk quietly with your heels lifted (6)

## DOWN

1. Cunning like a fox (3)
2. Owns; possesses (3)
3. Portable computer (6)
4. In the past, as in 'it was long ____' (3)
6. Device that gives out light (4)
7. Large wasp (6)
8. Whole numbers are _____ or odd (4)
9. Fluid used in a pen (3)
12. Six divided by six (3)
14. Have a meal (3)
15. Past tense of 14 down (3)

TIME

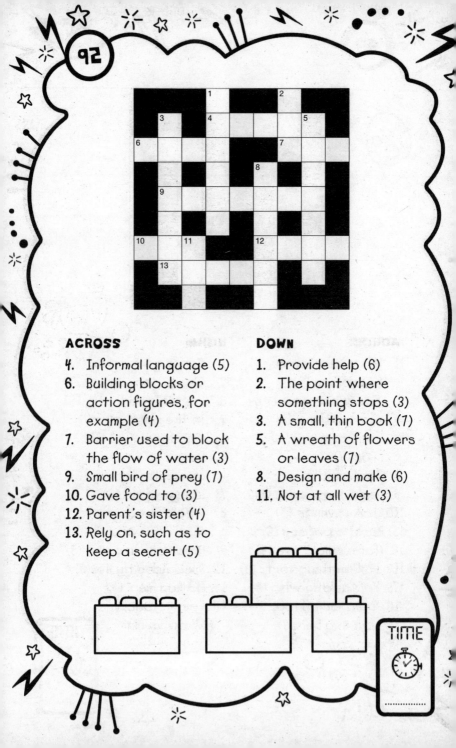

## ACROSS

4. Informal language (5)
6. Building blocks or action figures, for example (4)
7. Barrier used to block the flow of water (3)
9. Small bird of prey (7)
10. Gave food to (3)
12. Parent's sister (4)
13. Rely on, such as to keep a secret (5)

## DOWN

1. Provide help (6)
2. The point where something stops (3)
3. A small, thin book (7)
5. A wreath of flowers or leaves (7)
8. Design and make (6)
11. Not at all wet (3)

TIME

## ACROSS

1. At the summit of (4)
4. Evergreen tree with needle-like leaves (3)
5. Thick liquid used to fry food (3)
6. Toothed wheel (3)
8. Picture (5)
9. Repeatedly pester (3)
10. Jar cover (3)
11. Building where a family might live (5)
13. Hole in the ground (3)
15. A type of cereal (3)
16. Produce an egg, if you're a hen (3)
17. Very simple (4)

## DOWN

1. Region (4)
2. Someone who plays sports for a living (3)
3. Enrol in a club or society (4, 2)
4. Aircraft journey (6)
6. Crunchy green vegetable, often eaten raw (6)
7. Small but useful device or tool (6)
12. Fairy tale, "The _____ Duckling" (4)
14. Skating-rink surface (3)

TIME

## ACROSS

1. Untidy state (4)
4. Shelter used when camping (4)
7. Concluding part of a piece of music (4)
8. Sticky fastening material on a roll (4)
9. Card sent to one you love (9)
12. Young sheep (4)
14. A large group of soldiers that fight together on land (4)
16. Small insects (4)
17. Sound a car horn (4)

## DOWN

1. A computer made by Apple (3)
2. Bread that has gone hard is _____ (5)
3. Small, crawling insect (3)
5. Vehicle for hire (4)
6. In this location (4)
9. Really disgusting (4)
10. An arm or leg (4)
11. Garbage; heavily criticize (5)
13. Unopened flower (3)
15. Long-haired ox (3)

TIME

..............

## ACROSS

1. Device used to heat a room (8)
5. Writing device (3)
6. Not right (5)
8. Without any differences (9)
10. Young person (5)
13. Police officer (3)
15. Extinct prehistoric animal (8)

## DOWN

1. Tear (3)
2. Waltz or tango, for example (5)
3. Road-surfacing mixture (3)
4. Was in charge (3)
6. Magical woman (5)
7. Hairstyling stuff (3)
8. Cold and slippery (3)
9. Chocolate powder (5)
11. Having lived for a long time (3)
12. Metal container (3)
14. Average score at a golf hole (3)

TIME

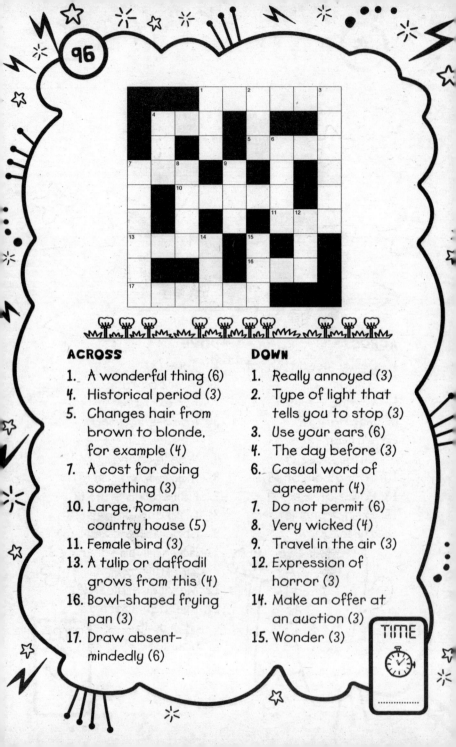

## ACROSS

1. A wonderful thing (6)
4. Historical period (3)
5. Changes hair from brown to blonde, for example (4)
7. A cost for doing something (3)
10. Large, Roman country house (5)
11. Female bird (3)
13. A tulip or daffodil grows from this (4)
16. Bowl-shaped frying pan (3)
17. Draw absent-mindedly (6)

## DOWN

1. Really annoyed (3)
2. Type of light that tells you to stop (3)
3. Use your ears (6)
4. The day before (3)
6. Casual word of agreement (4)
7. Do not permit (6)
8. Very wicked (4)
9. Travel in the air (3)
12. Expression of horror (3)
14. Make an offer at an auction (3)
15. Wonder (3)

TIME

## ACROSS

1. Imaginary ring around the middle of the Earth (7)
5. Round, green vegetable that grows in a 7 across (3)
7. A 5 across might grow in this (3)
8. Ruler of multiple countries (7)
9. Someone who cooks your food (4)
10. Small bird of prey (6)
13. Soak up liquid (6)
14. A hint (4)
16. Against the law (7)
18. Tennis serve winner (3)
19. The tip of a pen (3)
20. Europe and North America, contrasted with other countries (3,4)

## DOWN

1. The hope that something will happen (11)
2. Take your clothes off (7)
3. Tall plant with branches and leaves (4)
4. Say again (6)
5. The 'p' in m.p.h. on a vehicle dashboard (3)
6. A particular layout, such as of flowers (11)
11. Picture made by sticking together scraps of paper (7)
12. Shining strongly, like the sun (6)
15. Substance used for sticking things together (4)
17. Place that scientists work (3)

TIME

## ACROSS

1. You might receive this on your birthday (7)
5. Metal pole (3)
7. Tell a fib (3)
8. Not intended to be a joke (7)
9. Three times as much (6)
10. Sound that repeats back more quietly (4)
13. Barred animal enclosure (4)
14. Red playing-card suit (6)
16. Juicy fruit that's like a small peach (7)
18. When the tide goes out, it is said to ____ (3)
19. Took a seat (3)
20. Take air in and out of your lungs (7)

## DOWN

1. Elected people who run a country or town (11)
2. Late part of the day (7)
3. Without finding it at all hard (6)
4. Become in need of rest (4)
5. Word you shout to scare someone (3)
6. Being the main cause of something (11)
11. The flow of water in a river (7)
12. An insect with hard covers over its wings (6)
15. If you cut yourself, this might form over the wound (4)
17. Deep groove made by wheels (3)

TIME

## ACROSS

7. Living; existing (5)
8. Horse's whinny (5)
9. Activity where you sing along with words on a screen (7)
10. Narrow runner for use on snow (3)
11. Declares ready for business, like a shop (5)
13. Draw over something on to another sheet of paper on top (5)
15. Object used to cool yourself (3)
17. Spear once used to kill large sea creatures (7)
20. Something you sit on (5)
21. Female children (5)

## DOWN

1. Travel on foot (4)
2. Ferocious and aggressive (6)
3. Number represented by '0' (4)
4. Push an object into something else (6)
5. Lovingly touch someone with your lips (4)
6. Sacred place dedicated to a saint or god (6)
11. Somewhere people go to work at a desk (6)
12. A three-dimensional, perfectly round shape (6)
14. On a ship or plane (6)
16. Not far away (4)
18. Great anger (4)
19. The part of the face used for smelling (4)

TIME

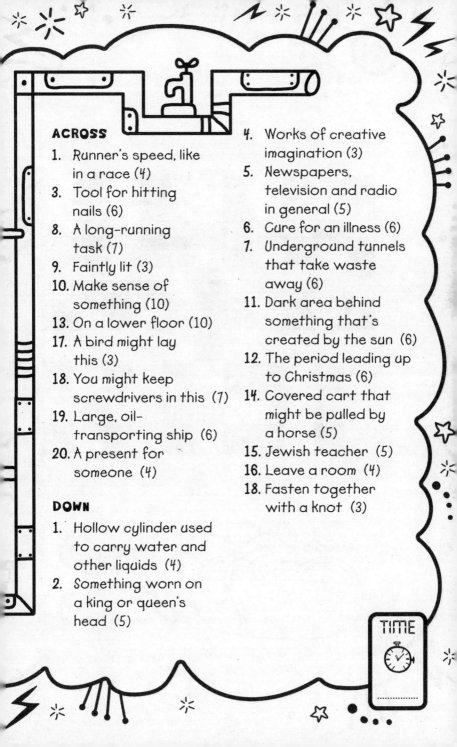

## ACROSS

1. Runner's speed, like in a race (4)
3. Tool for hitting nails (6)
8. A long-running task (7)
9. Faintly lit (3)
10. Make sense of something (10)
13. On a lower floor (10)
17. A bird might lay this (3)
18. You might keep screwdrivers in this (7)
19. Large, oil-transporting ship (6)
20. A present for someone (4)

## DOWN

1. Hollow cylinder used to carry water and other liquids (4)
2. Something worn on a king or queen's head (5)
4. Works of creative imagination (3)
5. Newspapers, television and radio in general (5)
6. Cure for an illness (6)
7. Underground tunnels that take waste away (6)
11. Dark area behind something that's created by the sun (6)
12. The period leading up to Christmas (6)
14. Covered cart that might be pulled by a horse (5)
15. Jewish teacher (5)
16. Leave a room (4)
18. Fasten together with a knot (3)

TIME

## ACROSS

1. A booking made to save a place (11)
7. Shout at someone (4)
8. Someone working on board a boat (6)
9. Makes a loud noise of surprise (5)
10. Get a ball into a goal, in sport (5)
13. One of usually four or more on a vehicle (5)
15. Entertain someone and make them laugh (5)
17. Fall to the ground and remain still, like snow (6)
18. Cereal ingredient in porridge (4)
19. A detailed test of your knowledge (11)

## DOWN

2. Short hair on your eyelid (7)
3. Oval-like shape (7)
4. A collarless, sleeveless garment worn on the top half of your body (4)
5. House made of ice (5)
6. Person trained to look after sick people (5)
11. Decayed grass and plant material, used to help other plants grow (7)
12. Italian rice dish (7)
13. Leftover parts; items that are not needed (5)
14. A minor actor who doesn't speak (5)
16. Cruel; unkind (4)

TIME

## ACROSS

1. Fierce storm with strong winds (9)
7. Having the same status and rights (5)
8. Sign used to indicate subtraction (5)
10. Group or society (4)
11. Pencil remover (6)
14. In a state of slumber (6)
15. Farm building where cows might be housed (4)
17. Strong claw, found on a bird of prey (5)
19. Crunchy green or red fruit (5)
20. A violent blowing apart of something, like a firework (9)

## DOWN

2. Not very common (7)
3. Something you are supposed to obey (4)
4. Photo-taking device (6)
5. Religious woman who lives in a convent (3)
6. Trader; someone who buys and sells things (8)
9. A person you do not know (8)
12. Soap for washing your hair (7)
13. House for a dog (6)
16. Rooms used for science experiments (4)
18. Not strict (3)

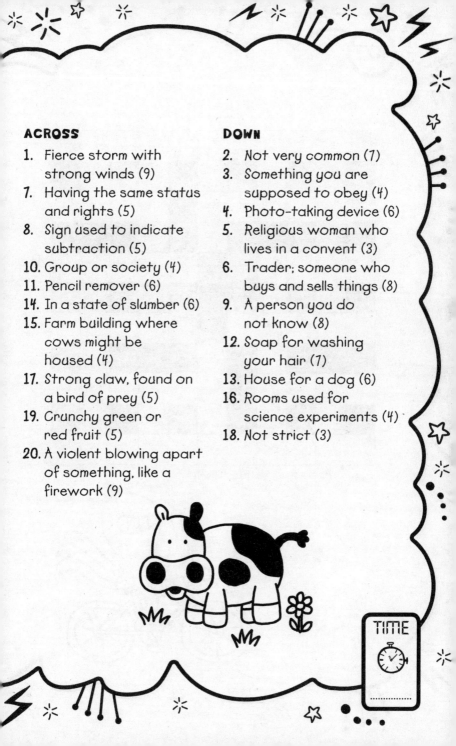

TIME

## ACROSS

1. Beneath the surface of the Earth (11)
7. Place where old objects are displayed (6)
8. It's used for keeping money in a shop (4)
9. The spiky part of a plant (5)
11. Priest (5)
13. Pedal a two-wheeled vehicle (5)
14. Cereal plant used to make flour (5)
16. Brainwave; clever thought (4)
18. The opposite of outside (6)
20. Clever; brainy (11)

## DOWN

2. Not well-behaved (7)
3. Lamb's mother (3)
4. Something that you play for fun (4)
5. Large bird that can run quickly but can't fly (7)
6. A score of zero (3)
10. Let go of something (7)
12. Leave behind (7)
15. Enter a number to make a phone call (4)
17. Wild animal's home (3)
19. Droop to a lower level (3)

TIME

## ACROSS

7. Get the necessary items, such as for a trip (5)
8. Cowboy contest (5)
9. Large seabird with a pouch in its beak for holding fish (7)
10. Another word for 'moose' (3)
11. Parent's brother (5)
13. The opposite of light, in terms of weight (5)
15. Rule that applies to everyone in a country (3)
17. Male who delivers mail (7)
20. Someone who writes software (5)
21. The gold medal position in a race (5)

## DOWN

1. Jump into the air (4)
2. The opposite of private (6)
3. A long story on a really big scale (4)
4. Tree limb (6)
5. Doing nothing (4)
6. Animal that is said to like eating bananas (6)
11. Open a door with a key (6)
12. Group of countries ruled by one person or country (6)
14. Regard someone with respect (6)
16. Walk through shallow water (4)
18. Not in any danger (4)
19. Short message or letter (4)

TIME

## ACROSS

3. Place where two bones connect (5)
6. Large, African ape (7)
7. Gather together into sets (5)
8. Green or purple fruit that grows on vines (5)
9. Buddy; anagram of 'lap' (3)
11. Pointy; not blunt (5)
13. Large stream (5)
15. Attempt (3)
18. Magic routine (5)
19. No longer a child (5)
20. Somebody who is temporarily visiting a place (7)
21. A book for keeping a day-by-day record of your life (5)

## DOWN

1. The position after third (6)
2. London Heathrow, for example (7)
3. South American wildcat that looks like a leopard (6)
4. Household item that's used to smooth clothes (4)
5. Enter letters using a keyboard (4)
10. Book-lending location (7)
12. Attractive; nice to look at (6)
14. Too much (6)
16. Difficult, like a tricky problem (4)
17. Edible fish that's sometimes bought in cans (4)

TIME

## ACROSS

1. You might shout this to ask for urgent assistance (4)
3. Drivers use these to slow down vehicles (6)
8. Green, leafy salad vegetable (7)
9. Limb connected to your shoulder (3)
10. Four-way junction in a road (10)
13. Glasses (10)
17. If you cut yourself, you may need first _____ (3)
18. Ancient Egyptian paper (7)
19. Short journey to deliver or fetch something, often for someone else (6)
20. A unit of computer memory storage (4)

## DOWN

1. Fraction sometimes written as 1/2 (4)
2. At some time in the future (5)
4. Small deer (3)
5. Bear-like Australian mammal (5)
6. Crispy Indian pastry filled with meat or vegetables (6)
7. The time of day when it gets dark (6)
11. Instructions for combining ingredients to make food (6)
12. Get away from (6)
14. Of a greater age (5)
15. Ahead of schedule (5)
16. Land surrounded by sea (4)
18. Metal dish with a handle, used for cooking (3)

TIME

## ACROSS

1. Science subject (9)
7. Christmas hymn (5)
8. Cloth used to make jeans (5)
10. Hut for storing gardening tools (4)
11. Not open (6)
14. A criminal fleeing justice (6)
15. Button used to turn the sound off on a TV (4)
17. Used a needle and thread (5)
19. Mozart's "The Magic Flute", for example (5)
20. Group of people living in one place (9)

## DOWN

2. The gathering of crops (7)
3. Not too harsh (4)
4. Seat put on a horse before riding (6)
5. Move quickly on foot (3)
6. Tool used for cutting paper (8)
9. To do with the Middle Ages (8)
12. A learner; someone who attends school (7)
13. Bicycle for two people (6)
16. Night-sky object that causes the tides (4)
18. Try to impress someone, especially in a romantic way (3)

TIME

## ACROSS

1. Large streams (6)
4. Watery ditch surrounding a castle (4)
8. Nocturnal bird of prey (3)
9. Repeated visual design (7)
10. The empty area that fills most of the universe (5)
11. Pinkish-yellow juicy fruit with furry skin (5)
13. February or March, for example (5)
15. Do very well at something (5)
17. Person who worked for someone, often in their home, e.g. a maid (7)
19. What you might call a male commanding officer (3)
20. Large town (4)
21. River crossing (6)

## DOWN

1. Underground parts of a tree (5)
2. The bad guy in a story (7)
3. Unit of currency in India (5)
5. The whole number between zero and two (3)
6. Position between ninth and eleventh (5)
7. To bring to a halt (4)
12. Blamed someone for something (7)
13. Enjoyable sounds made by instruments or voices (5)
14. High temperature (4)
15. Go into a room (5)
16. Big; of a greater size than average (5)
18. Go bad; decay (3)

TIME

..............

## ACROSS

1. The ability to think up new ideas (11)
7. Fire-breathing beast (6)
8. Specific day (4)
9. Unclean (5)
11. The holy table in a church, where the priest stands (5)
13. Once more (5)
14. The cost of buying something (5)
16. Level; smooth (4)
18. Mars and Neptune, for example (6)
20. Roughly correct (11)

## DOWN

2. Time denoted by 'a.m.' (7)
3. Joke (3)
4. The result of multiplying three by itself (4)
5. Young child who has just started to walk (7)
6. Not at home (3)
10. Bird's chirping noise (7)
12. From a very long time ago (7)
15. The very top of something (4)
17. The top half of your legs when sitting, where a cat might curl up (3)
19. A goal or target (3)

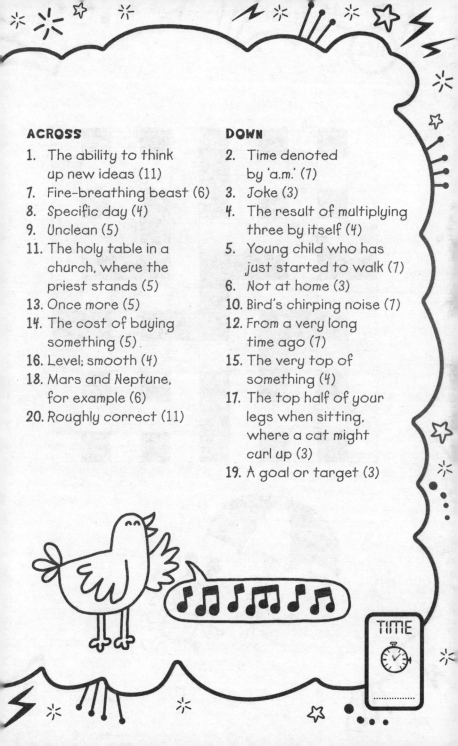

## ACROSS

7. Somewhere sports events take place (5)
8. Nut often gathered by squirrels (5)
9. Someone who teaches sports or fitness (7)
10. Sound made by a cow (3)
11. Everyday food substance made from flour (5)
13. The opposite of black (5)
15. The result of adding some numbers (3)
17. Sun umbrella used to provide shade (7)
20. Mistake (5)
21. A mix of cold, raw vegetables served as a meal or side dish (5)

## DOWN

1. Have a desire, as in 'I _____ to do this' (4)
2. Discussion (6)
3. Tell someone about a danger (4)
4. Make less wide (6)
5. Tiny, frothy bubbles made by soap (4)
6. Earnings (6)
11. Hoop target in a team sport (6)
12. Set out on a journey (6)
14. If you speak in a rude way to someone then you might do this (6)
16. Female horse (4)
18. Red flower that is a symbol of love (4)
19. The female equivalent of 'gentleman' (4)

TIME

## ACROSS

1. Pudding (7)
5. Enemy (3)
7. Going through, as in from one place to another (3)
8. Relating to water (7)
9. A character of the alphabet (6)
10. A small part missing from a cup, for example (4)
12. A narrow road for walking along (4)
14. Trip to see wild animals in their natural homes (6)
17. Fill with delight (7)
18. Two hours before midday (3)
19. Building set or a doll, for example (3)
20. One of your two nose openings (7)

## DOWN

1. The process of growing up and maturing (11)
2. First square on a board game (5)
3. What the white surface of teeth is made of (6)
4. A journey that visits several places (4)
5. Go and get (5)
6. Extremely good; out of the ordinary (11)
11. Prickly plant, often found in a desert (6)
13. Sticky (5)
15. Following on from (5)
16. Water that falls from the sky (4)

TIME

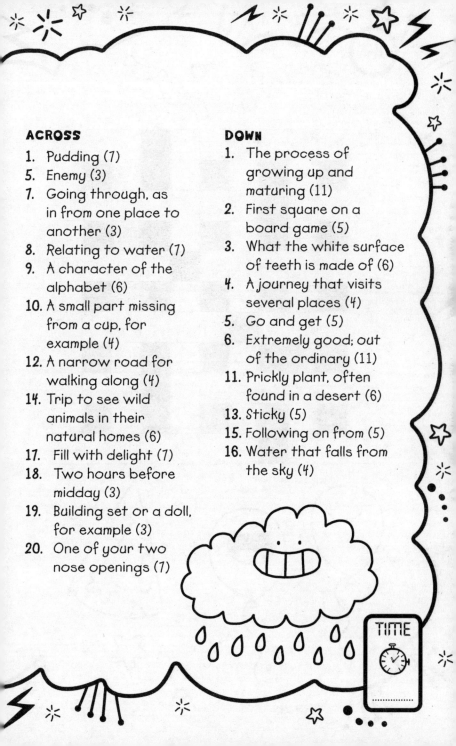

## ACROSS

1. Dried grape (7)
5. Mischievous creature (3)
7. Boy (3)
8. Person who is talking (7)
9. Something you might carry water in on a beach (6)
10. Currency used in many European countries (4)
13. Joins on to the end (4)
14. Between small and large in size (6)
16. Sickness (7)
18. Be the legal holder of (3)
19. Head movement used to signal 'yes' (3)
20. The absence of any sound (7)

## DOWN

1. A party for a special occasion (11)
2. Decreased (7)
3. Reply to a question (6)
4. Those people (4)
5. Liquid used for writing (3)
6. An event, such as a play, that takes place in front of people (11)
11. Mythical, one-horned animal (7)
12. A boat or ship (6)
15. The clear part of some spectacles (4)
17. Guided, as in a group of people (3)

TIME

## ACROSS

1. Vehicle for carrying injured people to hospital (9)
8. Describes how two lines meet, measured in degrees (5)
9. People who work in an office, for example (5)
10. Thin paper used for blowing your nose (6)
12. Country walk (4)
14. Large, decorative flower that's usually purple or yellow (4)
15. Young cat (6)
17. Very tall fairy-tale being (5)
18. A party with music to dance to (5)
20. Tornado (9)

## DOWN

2. Large cup (3)
3. Having a purpose (6)
4. This as well; too (4)
5. Horse-drawn carriage the Romans used for racing (7)
6. Bird in the pear tree? (9)
7. Period from noon to evening (9)
11. Dark green, leafy vegetable (7)
13. Glass area for looking out (6)
16. Mix a liquid (4)
19. The star that appears largest when viewed from Earth (3)

TIME

## ACROSS

1. The bones you move in order to eat (4)
4. It's worn inside a shoe (4)
7. McDonald's burger, Big ____ (3)
9. Record moving pictures (5)
10. Circular (5)
11. Permanent house covering (4)
12. Old fortified building (6)
14. Small, round object used to fasten clothes (6)
16. A piece of land (4)
19. Male duck (5)
20. Say (5)
21. Break a religious law (3)
22. Deliberate tangle in a piece of string or rope (4)
23. Not there any more (4)

## DOWN

2. Music and sound in general (5)
3. Haze (4)
4. Loud, shrill cry (6)
5. Find out how many there are of something (5)
6. All people (9)
8. An exciting journey or event (9)
13. Trustworthy (6)
15. Prepare for a sporting event (5)
17. Ancient Roman language (5)
18. A step on a ladder (4)

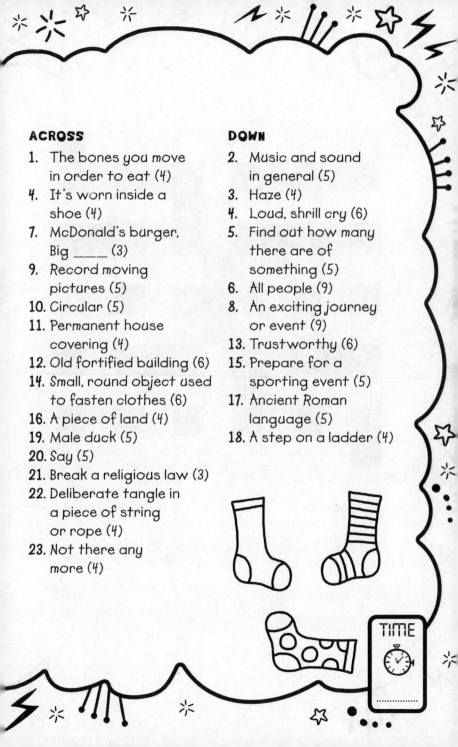

TIME

## ACROSS

1. Red fruit with seeds on the outside (10)
7. Private piece of information (6)
8. Bird kept for meat, such as a turkey (4)
9. At a higher level than (5)
11. Firm and crunchy (5)
13. Vegetables that might be green or broad (5)
14. Small, juicy fruit without a stone (5)
16. Deep, round dish (4)
18. Someone who uses a bow and arrow (6)
20. Say that something is better or worse than it really is (10)

## DOWN

2. Shake with fear (7)
3. The atmosphere all around us (3)
4. Word that means 'the two together' (4)
5. Sports umpire (7)
6. Evergreen tree with red berries (3)
10. What white ice cream often tastes of (7)
12. Snake (7)
15. Long, pointed animal tooth (4)
17. Have an obligation to repay something (3)
19. Motor vehicle (3)

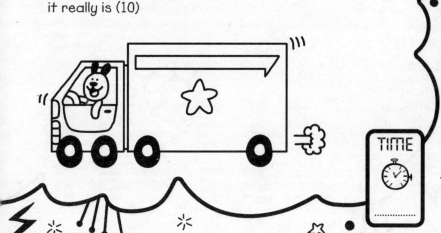

TIME

116

## ACROSS

7. Round vegetable with a strong smell (5)
8. White piano keys were once made of this (5)
9. Kitchen tool for browning slices of bread (7)
10. Small flap used to mark a page (3)
11. What you usually do at night (5)
13. In the countryside and away from town (5)
15. Not far above the ground (3)
17. Speak secretively (7)
20. Hard, solid rock; pebble (5)
21. Go up something, such as a hill (5)

## DOWN

1. A particular design of lettering (4)
2. Sailor who steals from other ships (6)
3. Small, mosquito-like fly (4)
4. Reflecting glass (6)
5. Wooden marker in the ground (4)
6. Percussion instrument that looks like a round metal plate (6)
11. If you jump into a swimming pool, you will make a _____ (6)
12. Dust-like substance (6)
14. Fix something that is broken (6)
16. Material made from sheep's hair (4)
18. A rash on your skin might do this (4)
19. A red, precious stone (4)

TIME

..............

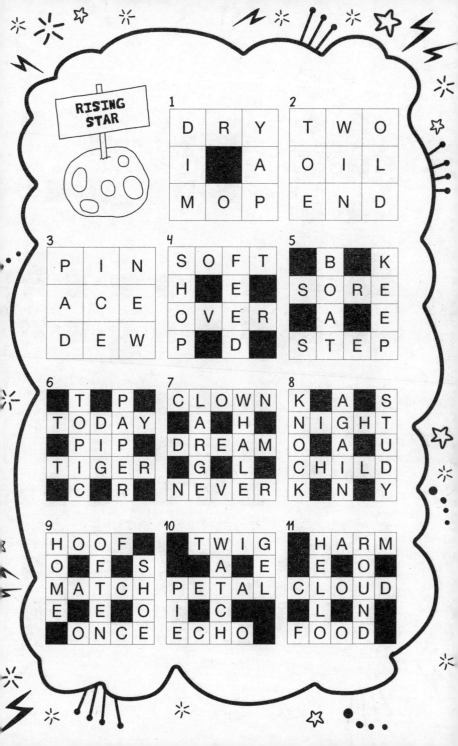

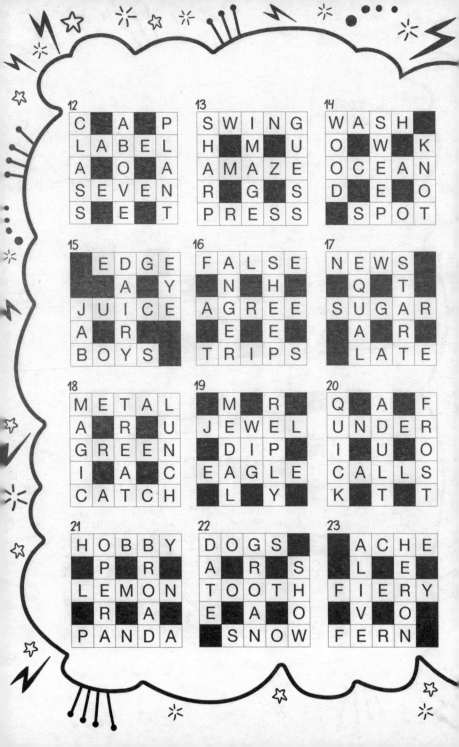

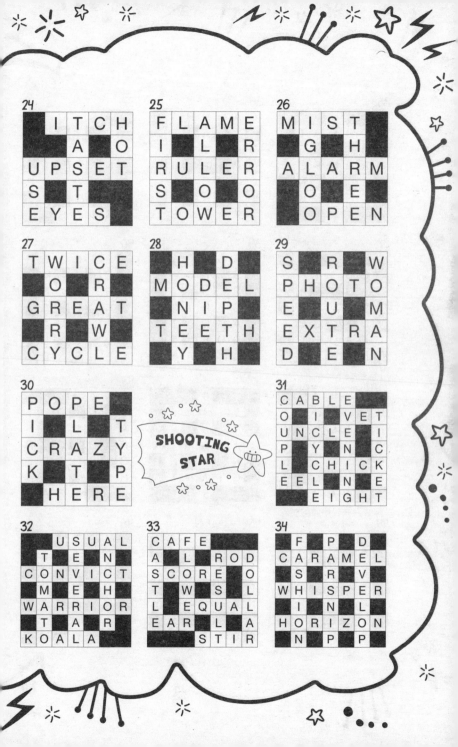

**24**

| | I | T | C | H |
| | A | | O | |
| U | P | S | E | T |
| S | | T | | |
| E | Y | E | S | |

**25**

| F | L | A | M | E |
| I | | L | | R |
| R | U | L | E | R |
| S | | O | | O |
| T | O | W | E | R |

**26**

| M | I | S | T | |
| | G | | H | |
| A | L | A | R | M |
| | O | | E | |
| | O | P | E | N |

**27**

| T | W | I | C | E |
| | O | | R | |
| G | R | E | A | T |
| | R | | W | |
| C | Y | C | L | E |

**28**

| | H | | D | |
| M | O | D | E | L |
| | N | | I | P |
| T | E | E | T | H |
| | Y | | H | |

**29**

| S | | R | | W |
| P | H | O | T | O |
| E | | U | | M |
| E | X | T | R | A |
| D | | E | | N |

**30**

| P | O | P | E | |
| I | | L | | T |
| C | R | A | Z | Y |
| K | | T | | P |
| | H | E | R | E |

SHOOTING STAR

**31**

| C | A | B | L | E | | |
| O | | I | | V | E | T |
| U | N | C | L | E | | I |
| P | | Y | | N | | C |
| L | | C | H | I | C | K |
| E | E | L | | N | | E |
| | E | I | G | H | T | |

**32**

| | U | S | U | A | L |
| | T | | E | | N |
| C | O | N | V | I | C | T |
| | M | | E | | H |
| W | A | R | R | I | O | R |
| | T | | A | | R |
| K | O | A | L | A | |

**33**

| C | A | F | E | | |
| A | | L | | R | O | D |
| S | C | O | R | E | | O |
| T | | W | | S | | L |
| L | | E | Q | U | A | L |
| E | A | R | | L | | A |
| | | S | T | I | R |

**34**

| | F | | P | | D |
| C | A | R | A | M | E | L |
| | S | | R | | V |
| W | H | I | S | P | E | R |
| | I | | N | | L |
| H | O | R | I | Z | O | N |
| | N | | P | | P |

**35**

```
. . M . . .
. C H E A T
C H . R . R
H A R M F U L
R . A . N .
T H I N K .
. . D . . .
```

**36**

```
C A M E R A .
. I . A . V .
B R O T H E R
. P . . . R .
C O N C E A L
. R . A . G .
T A R G E T .
```

**37**

```
. . S A U C E
. J . T . H .
C U S H I O N
. N . L . I .
S I L E N C E
. O . T . E .
F R I E S . .
```

**38**

```
. E . S . .
. G U I T A R
W A R . I . .
. R O Y A L .
D . . . G O T
L E A D E R .
N . . S . .
```

**39**

```
F A C T . . .
. B . H O W .
. R . U . I .
M O R N I N G
. A . D . T .
. D U E . E .
. . . . R A R E
```

**40**

```
. S I S T E R
. U . U . M .
P R I N C E .
. N . R . R .
A N I M A L .
. M . S . L .
L E G E N D .
```

**41**

```
S O C K S . .
C . O . O U T
H O T E L . W
O . T . D . E
O . A L I E N
L O G . E . T
. E A R L Y .
```

**42**

```
. . . B . . .
. S T A M P .
. T . N . R .
V I T A M I N
. N . N . N .
. G I A N T .
. . . S . . .
```

**43**

```
S N A P . . .
E . U . D O T
A N G L E . H
R . U . C . R
C . S H A P E
H U T . D . A
. . . D E A D
```

**44**

```
. F R U I T .
. D . E . G .
C E I L I N G
. L . A . O .
C E N T U R Y
. T . E . E .
R E A D Y . .
```

**45**

```
S L I D E S .
. E . E . H .
C O N C E A L
. P . . . T .
N A U G H T Y
. R . A . E .
D E P A R T .
```

**46**

```
. J . D . B .
G O R I L L A
. U . A . O .
P R O M I S E
. N . O . S .
R A I N B O W
. L . D . M .
```

# Crossword Grids

## 47
```
  S P I N E
F I T   L   A
O   A T L A S
S   T   N   I
S L I D E   L
I   O   S T Y
L U N G S
```

## 48
```
P A R T
  B   O N E
  S U   R
D O O R M A T
  R   I   S
B U S   E
      T U R N
```

## 49
```
C U B E
A   A   H O P
C E L L O   R
T   L   N   A
U   E N E M Y
S I T   S   E
      S T A R
```

## 50
```
      C
  S H O E S
S   L   W
B O U L D E R
  R   E   E
  Y A C H T
      T
```

## 51
```
  G A L A X Y
  L   I   E
C O M P O S T
  V   T
L E A T H E R
I   E   A
T U N N E L
```

## 52
```
      A   M
  P R I S O N
L I E   T
  L A U G H
  L   L E G
R O B B E R
  W   E
```

## 53
```
  S M A R T
S E E   C   U
U   A F T E R
M   G   R   K
M O U S E   E
E   L   S H Y
R U L E S
```

## 54
```
    S M I L E
  P   U   Y
D E S S E R T
  N   T   I
S C R A T C H
  I   R   S
B L A D E
```

## 55
```
  W   S   H
T E A C H E R
  L   O   X
A C R O B A T
  O   T   G
E M P E R O R
  E   R   N
```

## 56
```
A G E D
  R   E L F
  U   N   R
E M O T I O N
  P   I   Z
  Y E S   E
      T I N Y
```

## 57
```
W I D E
A   E   S E T
L I G H T   H
N   R   A   I
U   E N T E R
T I E   U   S
      N E S T
```

## 58
```
  S T R E E T
  P   O   A
W E D D I N G
  N   A
A D D R E S S
R   I   T
T R O P H Y
```

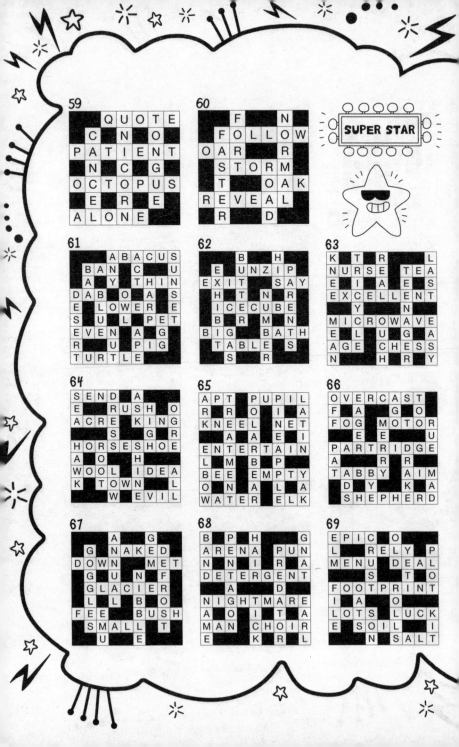

**SUPER STAR**

**59**

```
  Q U O T E
  C N   O
P A T I E N T
  N C   G
O C T O P U S
  E R   E
A L O N E
```

**60**

```
    F     N
  F O L L O W
O A R     R
  S T O R M
  T     O A K
R E V E A L
  R     D
```

**61**

```
  A B A C U S
B A N   C   U
A Y   T H I N
D A B O   A S
E   L O W E R
S U L   P E T
E V E N   A G
R   U   P I G
T U R T L E
```

**62**

```
    B   H
  E U N Z I P
E X I T   S A Y
  H T   N   R
  I C E C U B E
  B   R   M N
B I G     B A T H
  T A B L E S
  S       R
```

**63**

```
K   T   R       L
N U R S E   T E A
E   I   A   E S
E X C E L L E N T
    Y       N
M I C R O W A V E
E   L   U   G A
A G E   C H E S S
N       H   Y
```

**64**

```
S E N D   A
E   R U S H   O
A C R E   K I N G
    S   G   R
H O R S E S H O E
A   O   H
W O O L   I D E A
K   T O W N   L
    W   E V I L
```

**65**

```
A P T   P U P I L
R   R O   I   A
K N E E L   N E T
  A A   E   I
E N T E R T A I N
L   M   B   P
B E E   E M P T Y
O   N   A   L A
W A T E R   E L K
```

**66**

```
O V E R C A S T
F   A   G   O
F O G   M O T O R
E       E   U
P A R T R I D G E
A   R   R
T A B B Y   A I M
  D   Y   K A
S H E P H E R D
```

**67**

```
    A   G
  G N A K E D
D O W N   M E T
G U N   F
G L A C I E R
L L   B O
F E E   B U S H
S M A L L
  U   E
```

**68**

```
B   P   H   G
A R E N A   P U N
N N   I   R A
D E T E R G E N T
  A       D
N I G H T M A R E
A O   I   T A
M A N   C H O I R
E   K   R L
```

**69**

```
E P I C   O
L   R E L Y   P
M E N U   D E A L
  S       T O
F O O T P R I N T
I   A     O
L O T S   L U C K
E   S O I L   I
  N   S A L T
```

## 70

```
H A M . T E A R S
A . A . A . F . T
S I R E N . T A R
. M . G . E . A .
. S C A R E C R O W
H . L . R . R . N
E R A . I V O R Y
E . D . N . O . E
T H E R E . N O T
```

## 71

```
. . P O W D E R .
. T I E . A . A .
. O . W . S T U B
P E A . F U . B .
O . C L I M B . I
L . H . B . A N T
L I E D . D . U .
E . . U . O W N .
N I M B L E . . .
```

## 72

```
. . U . . I . . .
. P . S A I L S .
B Y T E . L A G .
R . F . S . T . .
A Q U A T I C . .
M . L . R . H . .
H I T . O X E N .
. D R I N K . L .
. Y . . . E . . .
```

## 73

```
Z . W . V . . R .
E R A S E . O R E
S . R . R . V . A
T E D D Y B E A R
. R . . R . . R .
P R O F E S S O R
L . B . X . E . I
A T E . A W A R D
Y . M . S . E . .
```

## 74

```
F L A M I N G O .
E . N . O . W . .
W O K . A D D E R
. L . R . . . A .
E V E R G R E E N
. E . U . M . . .
K N I F E . A I R
. I . I . I . A .
B U N G A L O W .
```

## 75

```
I R I S . C . . .
C . . T E A R . D
Y O G A . P A N E
. N . . . N . F E
G L A D I A T O R
O . R . . C . . .
N E C K . T U N A
E . H E R O . . I
. Y . . R E A D .
```

## 76

```
. . S O R R O W .
. F L U . A . I .
. R . E . Y A W N
Z O O M . D . D .
O . B E A R D . O
M . O . T . S O W
B E E F . O . D .
I . O . P O D . .
E X C E P T . . .
```

## 77

```
. . N . L . . . .
. Q . O N I O N .
N U M B . B O B .
A . O . I . O . .
R E D U C E D . .
R . Y . I . L . .
L E D . C H E F .
L O Y A L . S . .
. G . . E . . . .
```

## 78

```
S . L . R . . . F
A W A K E . P E R
I . N . S . R . O
L I G H T N I N G
. U . U . N . . .
C L A S S I C A L
H . G . A . E . A
A W E . V I S I T
T . E . S . E . .
```

## 79

```
A L P H A B E T .
D . A . O . U . .
D I N . C O R G I
I . O . . V . . .
A C C O M P A N Y
S . E . . P . . .
H E A R T . R O W
. V . A . O . O .
E N T R A N C E .
```

## 80

```
C L U B . I . . .
A . L U M P . X .
N I C E . P O O R
. A . . N . A . .
Y E S T E R D A Y
E . A . O . . . .
L O C K . A J A R
L . K I N D . U .
D . . S I G N . .
```

## 81

```
. . E M B E R S .
. S E W . E . T .
. K . E . D O O R
N I L . W . A . I
E . A G E N T . N
E . C . D . H U G
D U E L . M . R .
L . O . . I N N .
E X O T I C . . .
```

# 82

```
. A . H
. C . BAKER
CATS . . MEN
. U . U W . V
. TORNADO .
. I . D . L L
HOG . . LOVE
. NOISE . E
. . D . . T
```

# 83

```
S . A . M . C
MONEY . MOO
O . C . T . O L
GREYHOUND
. . S . N
ATTEMPTED
L . O . I . E
SIR . CHINA
O . . E . N F
```

# 84

```
DOC . ATLAS
A . A . P . I . P
BANJO . BAA
. A . L . R . D
VIDEOGAME
I . I . G . R
SPA . IDIOT
I . N . Z . A . O
TASTE . NAP
```

# 85

```
ABSOLUTE
P . P . S . E
EYE . HELLO
. L . A . . A
WALLPAPER
O . . P . E
NOISY . ANY
. F . E . C . E
FEATHERS
```

# 86

```
. . STATUS
. TOO . D . Y
. E . B . SWIM
GAS . L . E . B
A . PAUSE . O
M . O . G . PAL
BITE . A . R
L . M . GYM
EXCUSE
```

# 87

```
. P . F
. L . ALBUM
FOUR . ROB
. B . E . T . N
SANDALS
. T . T . T . T
WET . TREK
RADIO . R
. P . O
```

# 88

```
P . M . F . A
LLAMA . RUG
U . R . R . E . E
SCRAMBLED
. I . . A
SPAGHETTI
I . G . Y . I . T
CUE . MOVIE
K . . N . E . M
```

# 89

```
RAMP . A
U . INCH . E
BUZZ . TOAD
. Z . L . I
IMPATIENT
T . A . D
COST . EXIT
H . SOFA . O
N . LADY
```

# 90

```
CLARINET
U . T . E . A
POT . SWINE
I . O . A
ESCALATOR
L . V . I
FENCE . TOW
L . U . L . A
MATTRESS
```

# 91

```
. SCHOOL
ALL . A . A
G . Y . SLIP
HOE . I . A . T
O . VENOM . O
R . E . K . POP
NONE . A . N
E . . A . TEE
TIPTOE
```

# 92

```
. A . E
. B . SLANG
TOYS . DAM
O . I . C . R
KESTREL
L . T . E . A
FED . AUNT
. TRUST . D
Y . . E
```

# 93

```
. ATOP
J . FIR . R
OIL . E . COG
I . IMAGE . A
NAG . LID
U . HOUSE . G
PIT . G . RYE
. C . LAY . T
EASY
```

# 94

```
M E S S . A . . .
A . . T E N T . H
C O D A . T A P E
. L . X . . . R .
V A L E N T I N E
I . I . . . R . .
L A M B . A R M Y
E . B U G S . . A
. D . H O N K . .
```

# 95

```
R A D I A T O R .
I . A . A . A . .
P E N . W R O N G
. C . I . . C . .
. I D E N T I C A L
. C . C . . C . .
Y O U T H . C O P
. L . I . . O . A
. D I N O S A U R
```

# 96

```
. . M A R V E L .
. E R A . E . . I
. V . D . D Y E S
F E E . F . E . T
O . V I L L A . E
R . I . Y . . H E N
B U L B . A . . E
I . I . . W O K .
D O O D L E . . .
```

# 97

```
E Q U A T O R . P E A
X . N . R . E . . R .
P O D . E M P E R O R
E . E . R . E . . A .
C H E F . F A L C O N
T . S . B . T . O G .
A B S O R B . C L U E
T . I . I . G . L M .
I L L E G A L . A C E
O . A . H . U G . L .
N I B . T H E W E S T
```

# 98

```
P R E S E N T . B A R
O . V . A . I . O . E
L I E . S E R I O U S
I . I . N . E . P . P
T R I P L E . E C H O
I . N . Y . B . U . N
C A G E . H E A R T S
I . . S . E . R . E .
A P R I C O T . E B B
N . U . A . L N . L .
S A T . B R E A T H E
```

# 99

```
W . F . Z I K . S .
A L I V E . N E I G H
L . E . R . S S R .
K A R A O K E . S K I
. C . R . N . . B .
O P E N S . T R A C E
F . P . B . . . B .
F A N . H A R P O O N
I . E . A . A O . .
C H A I R . G I R L S
E . R . E . E D E .
```

# 100

```
P A C E . H A M M E R
I . R . S . R E E .
P R O J E C T . D I M
E . W . W . . I . E .
. U N D E R S T A N D
A . . R . H . . Y .
D O W N S T A I R S .
V . A . . D . A . E .
E G G . T O O L B O X
N . O . I . W . I .
T A N K E R . G I F T
```

# 101

```
R E S E R V A T I O N
. Y . L . E . G . U .
Y E L L . S A I L O R
. L . I . I . T . S .
G A S P S . S C O R E
. S . S . S . O . I .
W H E E L . A M U S E
A . X . M . P . O .
S E T T L E . O A T S
T . R . A . S . T .
E X A M I N A T I O N
```

# 102

```
. H U R R I C A N E
M . N . U . A . U .
E Q U A L . M I N U S
R . S . E . E . T .
C L U B . E R A S E R
H . A . K . A . H .
A S L E E P . B A R N
N . N . N . L . M .
T A L O N . A P P L E
. A . E . B . O . R
E X P L O S I O N .
```

# 103

```
U N D E R G R O U N D
. A . W . A . S . I .
M U S E U M . T I L L
. G . E . R . R . .
T H O R N . V I C A R
. T . E . C . B . .
C Y C L E . W H E A T
. E . D . E . D . N .
I D E A . I N S I D E
. E . S . A . A . O .
I N T E L L I G E N T
```

# 104

```
L . P . E . B . I . M
E Q U I P . R O D E O
A . B . I . A . L . N
P E L I C A N . E L K
I . . . C . . . . .
U N C L E . H E A V Y
N . . . M . . D . .
L A W . P O S T M A N
O . A . A . I . O .
C O D E R . F I R S T
K . E . E . E . E .
```

SUPERNOVA

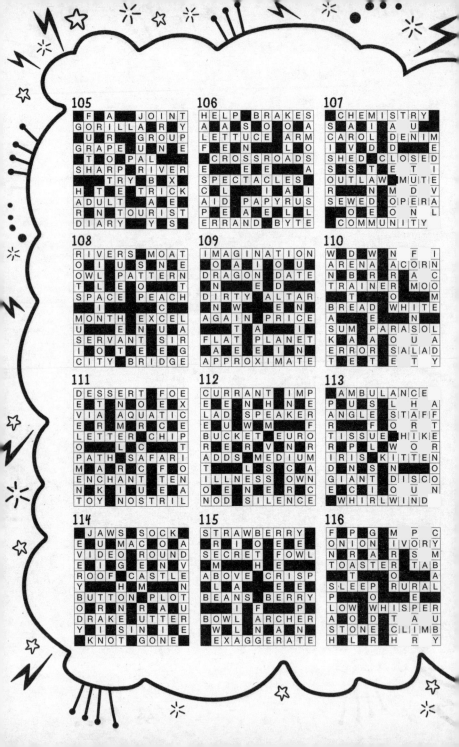

## 105
```
  F A   JOINT
GORILLA R Y
  U R GROUP
GRAPE U N E
  T O PAL
SHARP RIVER
    TRY B X
H E TRICK
ADULT A E
R N TOURIST
DIARY   Y S
```

## 106
```
HELP BRAKES
A A S O A A
LETTUCE ARM
E     N L O
  CROSSROADS
  E   E E
SPECTACLES
C L I A I
AID PAPYRUS
P E A E L L
ERRAND BYTE
```

## 107
```
 CHEMISTRY
S A I A U
CAROL DENIM
I V D D   E
SHED CLOSED
S S T E T I
OUTLAW MUTE
R N M D V
SEWED OPERA
 O E O N L
COMMUNITY
```

## 108
```
RIVERS MOAT
O I U S N E
OWL PATTERN
T L E O   T
SPACE PEACH
  I       C
MONTH EXCEL
U E N U A
SERVANT SIR
I O T E E G
CITY BRIDGE
```

## 109
```
IMAGINATION
O A I O U
DRAGON DATE
N     E D
DIRTY ALTAR
N W   E N
AGAIN PRICE
  T A   I
FLAT PLANET
A E E I N
APPROXIMATE
```

## 110
```
W D W N F I
ARENA ACORN
N B R R A C
TRAINER MOO
  T O O M
BREAD WHITE
A E     N
SUM PARASOL
K A A O U A
ERROR SALAD
T E T E T Y
```

## 111
```
DESSERT FOE
E T N O E X
VIA AQUATIC
E R M R C E
LETTER CHIP
O L   C T
PATH SAFARI
M A R C F O
ENCHANT TEN
N K I U E A
TOY NOSTRIL
```

## 112
```
CURRANT IMP
E E N H N E
LAD SPEAKER
E U W M   F
BUCKET EURO
R E R V N R
ADDS MEDIUM
T L S   C A
ILLNESS OWN
O E N E R C
NOD SILENCE
```

## 113
```
 AMBULANCE
P U S L H A
ANGLE STAFF
R O   R T
TISSUE HIKE
R P L W O R
IRIS KITTEN
D N S N   O
GIANT DISCO
E C I O U N
 WHIRLWIND
```

## 114
```
 JAWS SOCK
E U MAC O A
VIDEO ROUND
E I G E N V
ROOF CASTLE
Y H   M N
BUTTON PLOT
O R N R A U
DRAKE UTTER
Y I SIN I E
 KNOT GONE
```

## 115
```
STRAWBERRY
R I O E E
SECRET FOWL
M   H E
ABOVE CRISP
L A   E E
BEANS BERRY
I   I F P
BOWL ARCHER
W L N A N
EXAGGERATE
```

## 116
```
F P G M P C
ONION IVORY
N R A R S M
TOASTER TAB
T O A
SLEEP RURAL
P O E
LOW WHISPER
A O D T A U
STONE CLIMB
H L R H R Y
```